Arresting
the Arrester

Catching the Enemy
in His Own Trap

Arresting
the Arrester

Catching the Enemy
in His Own Trap

Enoch Adejare Adeboye

An imprint of Pneuma Life Publishing
Largo, MD

Copyright © 2002 Enoch Adejare Adeboye

ISBN 0-9711760-0-0

Christian Living Books, Inc.
An imprint of Pneuma Life Publishing, Inc.
P.O. Box 7584
Largo, MD 20792
301-218-9092
www.christianlivingbooks.com

Printed in the United States of America

Contents

Preface

The Bible records how Elisha frustrated the king of Syria because Elisha revealed his covert war plans to the king of Israel. The king of Syria got angry and decided to do something about Elisha. When the Syrian army arrived at Elisha's residence, he prayed that God would strike them with blindness. As soon as he finished speaking, they became mentally blind. He took them to the king of Israel. In summary, the Syrian army's mission was to arrest Elisha and take him to their king. Instead he turned the table around and arrested them with blindness.

This story is a classic example of arresting your enemy, who had plans to arrest you. God will deliver you from whatever or whoever is your "king of Syria," as long as you dwell in the secret place of the Most High God. That is the first step toward arresting your enemy. You will have to be confident and specific in your prayers to God, and you will surely praise God when He gives you victory over your enemies.

— Pastor E. A. Adeboye

Chapter One

Jesus:

---

the Winner

There is a lot of evil in this world. In fact, no matter who you are, you are going to have enemies.

Who is an enemy? Well, the enemy is not necessarily a "who." The enemy comes in many forms. It is anything that sets itself against your life. It is anything that is warring against you for no just cause. It could be anything from sickness or disease to your relatives.

But whatever is set against you, God is the One who will deliver you from it. He promises in Jeremiah 1:19 that the enemies will fight against you, but they will not overcome you. Psalm 34:19 states that the righteous have many afflictions, but God delivers him from them all. David said this in the Psalms:

> *The LORD is my light and my salvation; whom shall I*
> *fear? The LORD is the stronghold of my life–of whom*

Arresting
the Arrester

shall I be afraid? When evil men advance against me to devour my flesh, when my enemies and my foes attack me they will stumble and fall. (Psalm 27:1, 2)

Therefore, if you are going to defeat your enemy, the loser, the first thing you need to do is team up with a winner. That winner is Jesus. He is the One who cares about us. He takes care of all our needs. He offers salvation to every single person. And He will provide miracles to anyone who needs them.

In the Bible, the story of the king of Syria is a good illustration of how God helps us to defeat the enemy.

> *Now the King of [Syria] was at war with Israel. After conferring with his officers, he said, 'I will set up my camp in such and such a place.' The man of God sent word to the king of Israel: 'Beware of passing that place, because the [Syrians] are going down there.' So the king of Israel checked on the place indicated by the man of God. Time and again Elisha warned the king, so that he was on his guard in such places.* (2 Kings 6:8-10)

The king of Syria warred against Israel and planned an ambush for its king. He knew that once he got the head, the body would be captive. If you capture the head of state, you are in control of the nation. If you capture the head of a family, you already have the family. If you capture the head of a church, you already have the whole church. Therefore, we must constantly pray for our leaders so the devil will not ensnare them. As indicated in the Scriptures, there was a snoop in Israel. His name was Elisha. He exposed the battle blueprints of the king of Syria against Israel to the king of Israel.

2

God—Our Provider

Jesus: the Winner

The first word in verse 8, "Now," means this story is connected to a preceding story. It is either connected to the story of the floating ax head (2 Kings 6:5, 6), or it has something to do with the healing of Naaman, the Syrian army general in 2 Kings 5. If this story is linked with the story of the swimming ax head, it implies that immediately after Elisha ministered to a spiritual man, he ministered to a secular man. This tells us that God is not only interested in our spiritual well-being, but He is also interested in our secular well-being. In other words, He is interested in providing us with food, clothing and shelter. (See Matthew 6:9-11, John 21:3-12 and 1 Kings 19:4-8).

He makes these promises in several places in the Bible. One is in Matthew 6:26, which says: *"Look at the birds of the air; they do not sow or reap or store away in barns, and yet your heavenly Father feeds them. Are you not much more valuable than they?"* The One who feeds the birds of heaven shall feed you.

Another verse talks about clothing us:

> If that is how God clothes the grass of the field, which is here today and tomorrow is thrown into the fire, will he not much more clothe you, O you of little faith?
> (Matthew 6:30)

Furthermore, the Bible tells us that we shall not lack any good thing:

> The lions may grow weak and hungry, but those who seek the Lord lack no good thing. (Psalm 34:10)

Food, transportation, accommodations and clothing are all good things. God already has provided for our healing, according to Isaiah:

Arresting
the Arrester

But he was pierced for our transgressions, he was crushed for our iniquities; the punishment that brought us peace was upon him, and by his wounds we are healed. (Isaiah 53:5)

God also offers salvation to everyone, rich or poor. The same God that ministered to someone so poor that he had to borrow an ax also ministered to a king. God loves the whole world (John 3:16). Paul ministered to Lydia, a wealthy woman, in Acts 16, and she became born again. Acts 13:6-12 tells about the conversion of a governor. Luke 19:1-10 shows that salvation is also available to customs officials. In Matthew 8:5-11, there is salvation for military officers. John 3:1-8 shows that bishops, too, are offered salvation.

God is also the One who makes miracles happen. And the fact that Elisha ministered to a king after ministering to a prophet's son means that everybody needs a miracle. No matter how great you are, I believe you need a miracle. Jairus needed a miracle when death claimed his only daughter (Mark 5). He ran to Jesus for help. Jehoshaphat was a wealthy king, but when three kings aligned to annihilate him, he ran to God for a miracle (2 Chronicles 20:5-12). Whoever needs a miracle will get one.

Vengeance Belongs to God

This story can also be linked to the story of Naaman's healing. This seems to be the more probable progression. Naaman received his healing in Israel and went to present himself before the king of Syria. In return, the king got his soldiers ready to fight Israel. This clearly shows that the king of Syria was ungrateful. He decided to repay Israel with an invasion. He was the enemy.

4

Jesus: the Winner

If a man pays back evil for good, evil will never leave his house. (Proverbs 17:13)

If someone has paid you with evil for good, leave vengeance to God. His Word commands this. Proverbs 20:22 states, *"Do not say, 'I'll pay you back for this wrong!' Wait for the Lord, and he will deliver you."* Similarly, Romans 12:19 states: *"Do not take revenge, my friends, but leave room for God's wrath, for it is written: 'It is mine to avenge; I will repay,' says the Lord."* You also can pray for the one who has done you wrong.

> *For we know him who said, 'It is mine to avenge; I will repay' and again, 'The Lord will judge his people.' It is a dreadful thing to fall into the hands of the living God.*
> (Hebrews 10:30, 31)

As this verse states, it is a fearful thing to be handed over to God. We should never repay good with evil. When God is good to you, if you cannot thank Him, do not repay Him with evil. However, this was what Adam did to God (Genesis 3:12). Adam said it was the woman God gave him, Eve, who led him into temptation.

In the story of the king of Syria, he was an idol worshipper. He was a follower of the devil, so he did not understand goodness. There is nothing you can do to appease the devil (John 8:44, John 10:10); there is nothing you can do to appease opposition.

There is only one Deliverer from forces of darkness, the One at whose name every knee shall bow–Jesus. You cannot beg the devil. The only language he understands is that of violence.

> *Submit yourselves, then, to God. Resist the devil, and he will flee from you.* (James 4:7)

The devil is a loser.

Arresting
the Arrester

And there was war in heaven. Michael and his angels fought against the dragon, and the dragon and his angels fought back. But he was not strong enough, and they lost their place in heaven.

(Revelation 12:7, 8)

The devil was defeated, just as the king of Syria was defeated. Don't team up with the devil. Don't team up with a loser. If you do, you will become one yourself. If you team up with a winner, you will become a winner. Jesus is *the* winner.

What is the king of Syria in your life?

Deliverance from the Enemy

Isaiah 59:19 states that when the enemies come against you like a flood, the Almighty God will raise a standard against them. The Bible contains many examples of God delivering people from the enemy.

One is found in Mark 5:25-34. A woman had been bleeding continuously for twelve years. Whose fault was this? Is it a woman's fault that she menstruates? No. The devil just decided to war against the woman for no reason until she was reduced to nothing. But Jesus' touch healed her.

In Luke 13:10-13, a woman was bent over and could not walk upright. One day Jesus saw her and decided to release her. In fact Jesus Christ confirmed that she had been bound by Satan for twelve years. What was the woman's sin against Satan? Nothing. The devil messed up her gait for the fun of it.

Matthew 12:10-13 tells the story of the man with a withered hand. This withered hand "manhandled," as it were, the man for no just cause. One day, Jesus came into the temple, and the man got his miracle, even though the people protested this Sabbath day healing.

John 5:1-14 talks about a man who had been paralyzed for thirty-eight years. The enemy just decided to punish him. This man loved God and he wanted to worship Him, but the handicap limited him. He just laid in one spot, waiting for an angel to stir up the pool of Bethesda and a "chancy" dip in the water. It took the mercy of Jesus Christ to deliver him from the bondage of Satan.

In Mark 2:1-12, a man was paralyzed. He couldn't move his legs or his hands. What did he do to bring this on? Was his sin the greatest in the world? No. The enemy simply picked on him. This man found favor with God, and he was healed when his four friends brought him to Jesus Christ.

Mark 10:46-52 tells the story of blind Bartimaeus. Why did he become blind from birth? The enemy decided to attack him for no reason. The devil relishes reducing people to roadside beggars or non-entities.

Mark 5:1-15 tells the story of the madman from Gerasenes. More than a thousand demons claimed his life as their reserved residence. What did he do to get this sorely tormented? Deep within him, he wanted to worship God, but the demons wouldn't let him. One day, Jesus Christ passed by his "residence" - the cemetery and the man ran to Jesus and worshipped Him. He was delivered instantly.

Matthew 15:22-28 contains the story of a Samaritan woman who came to Jesus Christ, seeking deliverance for her daughter, tormented by the devil. The devil can possess your children to wage war against you. She got her miracle, though Jesus Christ called her a dog.

In Matthew 17:14-18, an epileptic child was brought to Jesus Christ by his father. The disciples could not heal the child until Jesus Christ came on the scene.

7

Arresting the Arrester

As these stories prove, no matter who or what represents the king of Syria in your life, as long as you dwell in the secret place of the Most High, the Lord will deliver you (Psalm 91:1-3).

Chapter Two

the Counsel of
the Lord Shall
Stand

When you team up with the Lord, He will stand victorious against any and all of your enemies and their followers.

In 2 Kings 6:8, before setting up camp, the king of Syria consulted his servants. This is what Satan does. He is one entity, but he has many demons as cohorts. In the Bible, whenever the children of God faced Satan and his cohorts, there was always a leader. It could be Pharaoh, Goliath or someone else. Usually, he had a host of others that were not named. When Satan wants to attack, he takes his followers along with him. He consults regularly with his demons.

It is these demons that you are to bind. You cannot bind Satan; you must resist him. If you bind demons correctly, they will remain bound unless you go back to set them free. According to the Word of God, as long as God is on your side, all those who gather against you will fall.

Arresting
the Arrester

If anyone does attack you, it will not be my doing; whoever attacks you will surrender to you. (Isaiah 54:15)

This shows you need not fear the devil if you belong to Jesus Christ. After all, *"greater is He that is in you than he that is in the world."* However, you cannot treat the devil as if he doesn't exist. Jesus said in John 8:12 that He is the Light of the world, and those who follow Him will not walk in darkness. Furthermore, when the king of Syria said such and such a place would be his camp, this means the enemy has a camp. Every child of God must never forget that just as there is light, there is darkness. Whether you believe it or not, the devil is very active.

You need to be aware of the devil because anybody who walks in darkness will stumble. Colossians 1:12, 13 says, one of the reasons you should always give thanks to God is because He has translated you from the kingdom of darkness to the kingdom of His Son.

To keep from walking in darkness, you must know where children of God should be found. Do not go into the camp of the enemy. There is no connection between darkness and light. Do not keep company with what the Bible calls the congregation of the dead (Proverbs 21:16). This includes the dead to Christ. There is a congregation of the living, which is alive, Bible-believing and tongue-talking. Stick close to that. This may be challenging at times.

When you begin to serve the Lord, you can be sure that there will be constant "satanic meetings" about you. But in the end, no one's purpose for your life but the Lord's will prevail.

> *The Lord foils the plans of the nations; he thwarts the purposes of the peoples.* (Psalm 33:10)

Proverbs further illustrates this point:

Many are the plans in a
man's heart, but it is the
Lord's purpose that pre-
vails." As God lives in you,
the counsel of the wicked against you will become nothing. (Proverbs 19:21)

Only the counsel of the Lord shall stand.

For it is written: 'I will destroy the wisdom of the wise;
the intelligence of the intelligent I will frustrate.'
(1 Corinthians 1:19)

When God is on your side, He has a supernatural strategy of
making every purpose of the enemy useless. The Lord's purpose is that those who do the will of God shall prosper in
whatever they do, and those who seek the Lord shall not lack
anything good. If doctors seem certain that based on your
medical history you will be infertile, tell them that the Lord's
plan for you is that your children will be like olive plants
around your table.

If medical experts tell you that you have a terminal illness, tell
them that is not the plan of the Lord. Instead, it is that you
shall live and declare the works of God. If economic experts
tell you that the macro-economic indicators in the country will
bankrupt your business, reject that counsel because it is not of
the Lord. The Lord's purpose is that you will prosper, be
healthy even as your soul prospers.

Joseph Believed God

The Bible contains many stories where God's purpose prevailed. In one, God told Joseph he would be the greatest in his
family. Joseph believed God, so he told his brothers. He told
them that they were going to bow down to him. His brothers
gathered and conspired against Joseph in Genesis 37:18-20.

Arresting
the Arrester

They threw him in a pit, but God made sure the pit was dry so Joseph would not die. People may delay the plan of God for your life, but they cannot prevent it. When you are with God, you will reach your God-given goals, whether the devil likes it or not.

After some time, Joseph's brothers decided to sell him into slavery. When he got to Potiphar's house, as a slave, he became the leader. The devil tried to use Potiphar's wife to destroy God's plan for Joseph, but he refused to fall into that trap. He went to prison for a crime he never committed, and when God took him out of prison, He gave him the throne as the Egyptian prime minister.

Whether the world likes it or not, one day, every knee shall bow at the name Jesus. Because you belong to Jesus Christ, a day will dawn soon when, at the name of Jesus, all your enemies will bow before you.

God's Plan for Moses

God's purpose also prevailed with Moses. Four hundred years before Moses was born, God told Abraham that one day, he would bring forth a man who would bring the children of Israel out of bondage in Egypt. Satan realized this, so he possessed Pharaoh and made him kill every boy born to the children of Israel. Before Moses was born, the devil was battle-ready for him. However, the counsel of the enemy could not stand. When Moses was born, God took over. He put him where nothing could reach him, right in the enemy's very own headquarters.

When Moses grew up, the devil tried again. Moses killed an Egyptian in the throes of immature rage and thought that his people would support him. The next day, he tried to mediate between two Israelites, and one of them rebuked him, reminding him of the murder. Moses became a fugitive for forty years, during which time it seemed God had forgotten him.

When Moses became eighty years old, it was time for God to execute His plan for Moses. God told Moses His will for his life must be done and sent him to Egypt to bring His people out of slavery.

Moses went as God sent him, but the Red Sea posed another problem. The Almighty God solved the problem by making Moses stretch his rod over the Red Sea, and it parted ways, so the Israelites could cross over. Every Red Sea blocking your way will part, in the name of Jesus Christ.

Then the devil brought the Amalekites to confront the children of Israel. Moses lifted up his hands and surrendered to God. God confirmed His counsel concerning him with victory for Israel.

David—The Chosen One

God's will also was done in David's life. God loved David's songs of praise to Him, and He decided to make him king. When the time was right, even David's Dad had a different opinion about David's future. This was evident in his indifference when prophet Samuel came calling to anoint one of his children as king (1 Samuel 16:11). But the man of God insisted on seeing David. Then God confirmed that he was the chosen one, and he was anointed (1 Samuel 16:13).

The devil went after David. He sent a lion and a bear to David, but David killed them. Next, the devil sent Goliath, and David killed the Philistine with his own weapon. Unrelenting, Satan decided to turn David's father-in-law against him. Saul rebuked Jonathan for being David's friend. Saul knew that God had cho-

Arresting
the Arrester

sen David to be king, just as your enemies know you will be great. They have done everything they can to bring you down, but they have failed. And they will continue to fail.

King Saul chased David from hills to caves, but he could not hurt him because it is the counsel of the Lord that will stand. When David got to the throne, his son Absalom planned a coup against him. However, God took care of Absalom just as He took care of Goliath. That is consistent with Isaiah 8:10, which says: *"Devise your strategy, but it will be thwarted; propose your plan, but it will not stand, for God is with us."*

God is with the righteous, no matter how warped the counsel of the wicked. If you are not born again, you cannot say God is with you. Therefore the counsel of the enemy against you will stand. If you come to Jesus Christ, repent and forsake all your sins, and let His blood cleanse you, then the counsel of the wicked against you will be canceled.

If you are already on the side of the Lord, you should thank God for what He has done in your life in the past and then prophesy that Satan's plans for your life shall not stand. It is the counsel of the Lord that shall stand.

Chapter Three

the Gift of

---

the Word of
Knowledge

When you are walking with God, from time to time, he will feed you information that will help you defeat your enemy.

Elisha is among those fortunate to have received the gift of the word of knowledge. He reveals this in 2 Kings:

> *The man of God sent word to the king of Israel: 'Beware of passing that place, because the Syrians are going down there.'* (2 Kings 6:9)

If it didn't come from God, how would Elisha, "the man of God," have known the plan of the king of Syria? How did the man of God know what was happening in another country? Man's knowledge is limited. In fact, the Bible states that we know in part, according to 1 Corinthians 13:9. We are told

Arresting
the Arrester

that we are yet to know as much as we should.

However, God is the all-knowing, omniscient God. The Bible states that in Acts 15:18 that known to God are all His works from the beginning of the world. God knows the end from the beginning. Revelations 1:8 discloses that the Almighty God is the Alpha and the Omega, the Beginning and the End. He knows everything that has happened, what is happening and what will happen. Psalm 139:7-10 states that God is everywhere at all times. David said in Psalm 139:1-12 that He even knows our thoughts because to Him darkness is as clear as day.

Whenever a man gets hooked up to God, God can give him a glimpse of what only He knows. He does this by the gift of the word of knowledge.

> *Now to each one the manifestation of the Spirit is given for the common good. To one there is given through the Spirit the message of wisdom, to another the message of knowledge by means of the same Spirit.*
>
> (1 Corinthians 12:7, 8)

God-Given Knowledge

The word of knowledge is a little fragment of knowledge God reveals to His servants.

How does God give this information? One way is through dreams. This does not mean you are to believe every dream you have. If you eat too much, you are likely to dream about food. If you have been fasting for a long time, you are likely to dream you are being fed. A thirsty man dreams of water. When a dream is repeated, however, you can be sure that God is telling you He wants to do something (Genesis 41:25, 29-32).

Another way God passes information to us is through the audible voice. God can speak to you, not necessarily through the physical ear, but through the spiritual ear. In Luke 5:1-6, Peter heard an audible voice.

Knowledge also comes as an inner vision. You can see it with the spiritual eye. This happened between Elisha and Gehazi in 2 Kings 5:25, 26.

Yet another channel of God-given knowledge is called the open vision. This comes without even sleeping. You suddenly see what God has done or wants to do. An example is in 2 Kings 6:15-17, where the enemy surrounded Elisha and his servant, and this prophet's personal assistant could not see the divine defense troops detailed to protect them. God later opened the servant's eyes to see the chariots of fire around them.

Let us briefly check out the advantages of the gift of the word of knowledge. When you know what God wants to do, it can deliver you from imminent danger and even destruction. An example is found in Genesis 7:4-16. Noah was saved from the floods because God had told him He was going to destroy the earth with them. He was able to receive deliverance for himself and his family because God forewarned him.

When you have this gift of prior knowledge of God's intentions, you will have peace in the midst of a storm. In Exodus 14:13, 14, when the children of Israel panicked at the Red Sea, Moses told them to relax and see God in action. This was because Moses knew what God would do to the Egyptians.

Moreover, when you are privileged to know the plan of God, it can get you out of debt. He can tell you what and what not to invest in. For instance, in 2 Kings 4:1-7, a debtor came to the man of God. She got a financial miracle because she listened to the man of God.

One of the most amazing advantages of the gift of the word of knowledge is that it can frustrate the enemy.

Arresting
the Arrester

But the word of knowledge can only work for you if you act on it. Two angels told Lot that they were sent to destroy Sodom and Gomorrah and that he needed to make a quick get-away. But his in-laws laughed at him. They could tell that destruction was heading in their direction, yet they perished in it. In 1 Samuel 3, God told Eli through Samuel that He was angry with him and his children. Eli said God could do whatever He liked.

When you hear the word of knowledge and you do nothing about it, you are missing a blessing. When you do act, the extent to which you apply the knowledge revealed to you determines the extent of your benefits from it.

Jesus told Peter to throw all his nets into the sea, but he threw only one. This determined the number of fishes his net could handle. Recall that he had to call for help from other fishermen when his small net could not handle his big, miraculous catch. Another example is the woman who inherited debts from her husband (2 Kings 4:1-7).

God's Warnings

There is a word of knowledge that God has given to every Christian. He says whatever we give Him, He will return to us in multiples of one hundred. Yet when it is time to give to God, we only think of what we are giving and not the hundred-fold return. The Almighty God gives us knowledge in the form of warnings in the Bible. In 2 Kings 6:9, the man of God told the king of Israel to "beware." This was a warning to be aware. Unfortunately, many of us ignore warnings from God to our own detriment. They can be summed up in three words: Beware of sin.

If we listen to God's warnings, it can help us fight the enemy. The story in John 5:1-14 is a good example. It tells of a man who had been ill for thirty-eight years. When Jesus healed him, He told him to go and sin no more. Jesus has not healed many people today because they have not made up their minds to forsake sin. In Romans 6:1, 2, God asks us if we can continue in sin and expect grace to abound. God forbid! If you do not make up your mind to forsake sin, you are asking for trouble. You may continue to suffer for a long time to come until you forsake sin.

Another warning is found in Proverbs:

> He who conceals his sins does not prosper, but whoever confesses and renounces them finds mercy.
>
> (Proverbs 28:13)

We must listen to these warnings, as well as all other avenues of communication from God, if we want total victory over our enemies.

Chapter Four

Who is
on the Lord's
Side?

When God links you with a true prophet of God, although they are few, you must thank God for it and pay attention to whatever he tells you. If you do, according to Jehoshaphat in 2 Chronicles 20:20, you will prosper.

Jesus also says this to His disciples:

> He who receives you receives me, and he who receives me receives the one who sent me. Anyone who receives a prophet because he is a prophet will receive a prophet's reward, and anyone who receives a righteous man because he is a righteous man will receive a righteous man's reward. (Matthew 10:40, 41)

This saved the king of Israel, who listened to the prophet Elisha and acted on his words.

Arresting
the Arrester

So the king of Israel checked on the place indicated by the man of God. Time and again Elisha warned the king, so that he was on his guard in such places. This enraged the king of [Syria]. He summoned his officers and demanded of them, 'Will you not tell me which of us is on the side of the king of Israel?' 'None of us, my lord the king,' said one of his officers, "but Elisha, the prophet who is in Israel, tells the king of Israel the very words you speak in your bedroom.

(2 Kings 6:10-12)

Thanks to Elisha, the king of Israel escaped the ambush of the king of Syria. The king of Syria then called another meeting and planned two more attempts to ambush the king of Israel, but they failed. This kindled his suspicion. He interrogated his servants to find out which of them was the double agent. One of them was bold enough to point out the perceptive power of the prophet in Israel who knew everything the king was doing in his bedroom. He said the prophet was Elisha.

The king of Israel could have been in trouble if he had not listened to the prophet. He would have ended up a prisoner of war or a corpse.

Listen to the Prophet

When a man of God tells you that it will be well with you, you better say, "Amen." Many of us have lost miracles because we do not believe the true prophets of God. When he says all is well, we still insist that he lay hands on us before we receive our miracles. By doing this, we are cursing ourselves by saying nothing will happen unless he lays hands on us.

The king of Israel avoided the ambush sites the man of God told him about and saved himself there over and over again.

We all know that only the Almighty God, no pastor or prophet, can deliver and make you safe.

There is no wisdom, no insight, no plan that can succeed against the Lord. The horse is made ready for the day of battle, but victory rests with the Lord.
(Proverbs 21:30, 31)

The Lord your God is with you, he is mighty to save. He will take great delight in you, he will quiet you with his love, he will rejoice over you with singing.
(Zephaniah 3:17)

We have an awesome God, and He is able to deliver from any enemy, any number of times.

Salvation to the Uttermost

The fact that the king of Israel was delivered many times tells us that the Almighty God can save not once, not twice, but all the time. The Bible states that He is able to save to the uttermost. He can deliver you today, and if the enemy tries tomorrow, He will deliver you again because He never gets weary. He sees everything, everywhere, at all times, and He is ready to deliver you for as long as you allow Him.

He who dwells in the shelter of the Most High will rest in the shadow of the Almighty. I will say of the Lord, 'He is my refuge and my fortress, my God, in whom I trust.' Surely he will save you from the fowler's snare and from the deadly pestilence. (Psalm 91:1-3)

As long as you dwell with God permanently, your enemies will fail over and over, just like the king of Syria failed again and again.

Arresting the Arrester

And this will take its toll on your enemies. The Bible records how the heart of the king of Syria was sorely troubled. This will happen to our enemies–they will end up with their hearts severely troubled. Why? Isaiah 48:22 has the answer: *"'There is no peace,' says the Lord, 'for the wicked.'"*

God decreed that the wicked would have no peace. Why? The answer to this is in Proverbs:

> The wicked man flees when no one pursues, but the righteous are bold as a lion. (Proverbs 28:1)

In other words, the wicked man runs from his own shadow. However, when you are in Jesus Christ and you do not war against any man, somehow deep within your heart, you know that if anyone raises a finger against you, the Lord of host will deal with that finger and the owner of it. This is why the Bible says the righteous are as bold as a lion, but the wicked man has no peace. The righteous man has nothing to fear.

> Surely he will never be shaken; a righteous man will be remembered forever. He will have no fear of bad news; his heart is steadfast, trusting in the Lord. His heart is secure, he will have no fear; in the end he will look in triumph on his foes. (Psalm 112:6-8)

Romans 8:31 asks, If God is for us, who can be against us? However, Isaiah states:

> Surely the arm of the Lord is not too short to save, nor his ear too dull to hear. But your iniquities have separated you from your God; your sins have hidden his face from you, so that he will not hear. (Isaiah 59:1, 2)

If there is no sin in your life, no matter how many enemies you have, they will not be able to hurt you.

Who's on the Lord's Side?

Lord's Side?

Examine your life. Who is the enemy within you? If you know you are not doing the right things, you better repent. 2 Kings 6:11 asks who was on the side of the king of Israel. Israel has only one king, and His name Is Jehovah. Thus, the question being asked is, Who is on the Lord's side?

People who are on the Lord's side can do supernatural things. Enemies can never prevail against them. In Genesis 14:14-16, Abraham heard that Lot and his family had been captured. Abraham said he would pursue and destroy the enemy, as long as the Lord lives. Abraham caught up with the enemy and recovered all from the enemy. You, too, will recover all that the enemy has stolen from you, so long as you are on the Lord's side.

David was on the Lord's side, too (1 Samuel 17). When David came face-to-face with Goliath, David told him his weapons of war were sealed in the name of the Lord of hosts. At the end of the day, the mountain called Goliath was leveled. If you are on the Lord's side, all the mountains blocking your path to progress will be removed. Your Goliath will bow and lose his head.

Daniel was also on the Lord's side (Daniel 6). Daniel was thrown into the lion's den, but the lions rejected dinner this time. God intervened because Daniel was on the Lord's side. If you are on the Lord's side, the lions of this world cannot eat you. As Daniel gained his freedom, the Lord ensured him that his enemies died in his place:

> At the King's command, the men who had falsely accused Daniel were brought in and thrown into the lions' den, along with their wives and children. And before they reached the floor of the den, the lions overpowered them and crushed all their bones.

(Daniel 6:24)

Arresting
the Arrester

Anyone who says a child of God should not prosper or make progress will perish.

How do we know those who are on the Lord's side? Look also at the examples set by Abraham, David and Daniel. In Genesis 14:18-20, Abraham paid the tithes of all his increase as soon as he returned victorious from the war during which he gathered a lot of booty from the enemies. Some say tithe is in the law and that we are now in the time of grace. That is wrong. Paying tithes came before the law. The law came with Moses; paying tithes came through Abraham.

If you are on the side of the Lord, you will pay all your tithes, and you will not ask God for the receipts or help Him spend it. When you pay your tithes, God should not have to thank you because you are merely doing your duty. Nonetheless, He said if you pay your tithes, He would open the windows of heaven and bless you so much that you would not have enough room for it. He says if you do not do it, you become a robber and the enemy within.

Protect God's Name

In the case of David, why did he decide to fight Goliath? He said Goliath blasphemed the name of the Lord of hosts. Those who are on the Lord's side will do everything to protect God's name.

Instead of doing this, however, many of us insult the Lord's name by the way we behave. What do people think of you? What is your testimony? What kind of life are you living? Your lifestyle will show people that you belong to Jesus Christ. Once you become born again, you must desist from those things that can put down the name of Jesus.

Our third example is Daniel. When the people of the world (in Babylon) examined Daniel, they concluded that there was no fault in him. Daniel was a prayer warrior. He defied the king's order not to pray. On the other hand, some of us do not pray over our food. In public, many of us do not pray because we don't want to be called fanatics. But if you are on the Lord's side, you cannot hide it. The city set upon the hill cannot be hidden.

Real prayer is principally worship. God is a spirit, and those who worship Him must worship Him in spirit and in truth. When you want to really pray, ninety-nine percent of the prayer time should be spent in worship. If you praise Him for what He has done, He will do more. If you are on the Lord's side, you will be able to stand up and say, without any shadow of doubt, that no weapon fashioned against you shall prosper. Can you imagine an opponent that no weapon can destroy? If you have such an enemy, you should be afraid of him or her. This is what you are expected to be to the enemy.

Not only are we to be indestructible, it is our heritage to condemn every enemy that rises up against us. Isaiah 54:15 states that our enemies will gather against us, but they shall fall. This Word of God is forever settled. Our enemies shall fall, by divine decree. Once you decide to be the Lord's one hundred percent, you do not have to worry about enemies anymore. Deuteronomy 28:7 assures us that God will cause our enemies to be smitten before us. They will come against us one way and flee from us in seven ways.

The king of Syria was told that Elisha was the terror. The devil should be able to say this about you. Actually, it was the God of Elisha that was at work. Elisha was a Holy Ghost carrier. This is what God wants you to be.

How many of us would like to be like Elisha? How many us would like to be a one-man terror squad to the devil? How many of us want to be great? It is the will of God that we should be great.

Arresting
the Arrester

The Lord will make you the head, not the tail. If you pay attention to the commands of the Lord your God that I give you this day and carefully follow them, you will always be at the top, never at the bottom.
(Deuteronomy 28:13)

Can you be as great as Elisha was? Matthew 11:11 acknowledges that the Baptist also was great, but not as great as the least in the kingdom of heaven. John the Baptist was greater than Elisha and anyone in the Old Testament. Any born-again member of the kingdom of God is greater than John the Baptist. If you are born again by the divine decree of the Almighty God, you will be greater than Elisha.

From now on, you must thirst for greatness. The Word of God states that blessed are those who hunger and thirst after righteousness because they shall be filled. Jesus also said if any man thirsts earnestly, he should come to Him.

Chapter Five

Victory in
Spiritual
Warfare

As we join with Jesus to defeat our enemies, we must never become discouraged or give up on our goals. This will prevent our victory, our miracle. In spiritual warfare, it is also important to make a difference in our lives and to act wisely.

Even after a few defeats, the king of Syria didn't get discouraged.

> 'Go, find out where he is,' the king ordered, 'so I can send men and capture him.' The report came back: 'He is in Dothan.' Then he sent horses and chariots and a strong force there. They went by night and surrounded the city. (2 Kings 6:13, 14)

Arresting
the Arrester

The king of Syria told his soldiers to go and spy out Elisha's location. This means he was not discouraged, having been defeated about three times.

However, many people do get discouraged just as they are about to get their miracles. This can be devastating because anyone who gets discouraged will never reach his or her goal.

The spies came back with the report that they could not possess the Promised Land because the city was walled and the people in there were giants, even after God backed them up all the way through the hassles they encountered in the desert. The spies were discouraged and thought it would be better to go back to Egypt. God told them if they could not go on, they would die in the desert.

Discouragement is Expensive

Discouragement is something you cannot afford to allow in your life. If you refuse to be discouraged, your victory will be a given.

This was the case in 1 Samuel 30:1-6, 18. When David and his soldiers returned from war with the Philistines, he discovered that the Amalekites had overrun their city, making prisoners of all their wives and children. They were broken-hearted, and they wept. David couldn't hold back his tears. It wasn't long before the soldiers went buck-passing and ranted against David. They were depressed, but David encouraged himself in the Lord. He lifted up his eyes unto the hills, and help came from God. God told him to pursue the enemies, and he became victorious and recovered all that the enemies took away from Ziklag.

We also should not get discouraged and quit because, as Hebrews 10:38, 39 states, if any man draws back, God shall have no pleasure in him. God has no pleasure in quitters. Furthermore, in Luke 9:62, Jesus said that anyone who has laid his hands upon the plow and then looks back is not fit for the kingdom of heaven. Once you say you will go forward, you must never look back.

You may say you have prayed, and nothing has happened, or that God has said "no" to your request. Still, this isn't grounds enough to feel discouraged. A good illustration is in John 2:1-11. At the wedding in Cana, Galilee, Jesus seemed initially unconcerned when the wine finished. His mother hinted the caterers to do whatever He directed them to do. This is because she was sure He would help. After she appealed to Jesus to do something, had she been discouraged, no miracle would have been performed.

In fact, His Word indicates there are no grounds for getting discouraged. In Luke 18:1-7, Jesus said men must always pray, without giving up. He also told the story of a judge who had no regard for human or godly standards, but who changed his mind after the persistent plea from a poor woman. If Bartimaeus had not been insistent in his appeals to Jesus in Mark 10:48, he would have missed his miracle. There is also the story of the Samaritan woman who came to Jesus to get her daughter healed. Jesus did not answer her until she persevered. Even the disciples who could have helped her asked Jesus to send her away. She could have been discouraged when Jesus called her a dog. But she was adamant and got her miracle.

It is easy to go forward when there is nowhere else to go. But when you have a benefactor or fallback position apart from Jesus Christ, you can easily give up on pressing forward.

It is a natural choice to press on with Jesus when you discover that there is no helper like Him. Any problem that has brought you to the knowledge of Jesus Christ has brought you

31

Arresting
the Arrester

to the Ultimate Helper. If Jesus cannot help you, nobody can. He can help because all powers in heaven and on earth have been given to Him.

One Step Closer to Success

If you are contemplating giving up, think about this: What if your next effort brings you success? It may be the final effort that would lead you to your answer. Even if it is not the final one, at least it is one step closer to success. Each time you make an effort, you will get a step closer to victory. Anyone who refuses to quit will succeed eventually with God on his side. The only people who will not quit but will still fail are those who are set against God.

If you are persistent in seeking victory, it will help you to become somebody who cannot be ignored–just like Elisha. This is God's plan for all areas of your life.

When the king of Syria was told that Elisha was his enemy, he had two options: ignore him or fight him. He chose the second option. He knew Elisha was not a man to ignore. The Bible contains many other examples. In one, Genesis 26:12-14 showed how Isaac waxed so great that the Philistines envied him. They could not ignore him because God blessed him. We are of the seed of Abraham, just as Isaac, so this is the plan of God for our lives, too. Take note, however, that Isaac was a sower and a giver.

In another example, Acts 9:36-42 tells the story of the death of Dorcas, another great giver. Because she was someone who could not be ignored, the people refused to accept her death. They testified of the good things she had done. Peter called on God to raise Dorcas, and God commanded death to give her up.

32

A third example is in Judges 4:1-10, which tells the story of Deborah and the Israelites. The children of Israel were in trouble, and Deborah spearheaded the solution to the problems. She sent for a warrior to get the soldiers together. The war general said they would go to war only if Deborah went with them. She mobilized warriors to God-ordained victories as the spiritual warrior of her time.

Your life should have a purpose, too. Don't be ignored. Make a difference. Let your life be like that of Rehab who brought salvation to her household. Do something with your life that would change your generation for good.

You also need wisdom to fight spiritual warfare. The fact that the king of Syria sent out spies against Elisha implies that wisdom is an indispensable constant in the spiritual warfare equation. Other Scriptures address wisdom. Ecclesiastes 9:16 states that wisdom is better than strength. Ecclesiastes 9:18 states that wisdom is better than weapons of war. If you have weapons, and you lack wisdom, you will fail. Ecclesiastes 7:12 states that wisdom is a defense.

Another key to success in spiritual warfare is to watch your tongue. This is because the success of a spy mission depends on what is heard more than what is seen. When Joshua sent spies into Jericho, their report was based on what they heard from Rehab. She said everybody's heart had melted because they knew that the children of Israel were set to destroy Jericho and that their God is a great God.

Your enemies will not know your secret unless you tell them. So heed the wisdom in Proverbs 18:7, which states that the mouth of a fool is his destruction. Similarly, Ecclesiastes 10:12 explains that the lips of a fool will swallow him. Proverbs 29:11 also speaks about this. It says a fool will say all that is on his mind, while a wise man will keep his lips in check.

33

Arresting
the Arrester

*He who guards his mouth
and his tongue keeps him-
self from calamity.*

(Proverbs 21:23)

This is important advice, as many of us have destroyed our
prospects by talking too much. Many men of God are not
where they are supposed to be because they talk too much.
Many businesses have collapsed because their owners talked
too much. There are many sisters who would have been married today but as soon as a brother came, they told everybody,
and things changed. Do not give your testimony until it is
complete. Learn to control your tongue.

Lessons in Spiritual Warfare

In summary, the king of Syria has taught us seven lessons in
spiritual warfare.

The first one is that we must have an ultimate goal. If you don't
know where you want to go, you may go around in circles and
think you are making progress. The king of Syria had an ultimate goal–to subjugate Israel under his kingdom–and he pur-
sued it. My goal is to go to heaven, and I am going to take
many people with me.

Second, you must devise a method of reaching your goal by
using wisdom, rather than strength. The Syrian king knew
there was no need to go to war with Israel. All he needed was
to capture their king.

Third, if you find yourself failing again and again, you should
seek counsel and find out what is wrong. The Bible admonishes us to make war with good advice.

The fourth lesson is that anyone who befriends your enemy is
your enemy. Elisha was the friend of the king of Israel. The
king of Israel was the enemy of the king of Syria.. James 4:4
clearly states that friendship with the world is enmity with

God. If you befriend the world, you can be sure that you are God's enemy.

The fifth lesson is that you must properly locate the mountain standing in your way. The Word of God encourages you to speak to "this mountain," meaning a specific mountain. You must know with what you are contending. Before you can say God should arise and His enemies scatter, you have to be sure that you are not one of the enemies of God. Be sure that you are not your own enemy number one.

The sixth lesson: We must never lose hope, no matter how big the mountain. To the king of Syria, Elisha was a very big mountain. Your mountain will have to move. God knows the foundation of your problem, your mountain, and He will uproot it (Psalm 90:1, 2).

Finally, when you go into spiritual warfare, be sure you are not fighting against God. If you are fighting God, you will lose. On the other hand, with God on your side, you will win all your battles. If God is on your side, you will look for your enemies, and you will not find them.

Demons Tremble

This is because God will make your enemies disappear. Demons recognize and tremble at the name of Jesus Christ, as stated in James:

> You believe that there is one God. Good! Even the demons believe that—and shudder. (James 2:19)

At the name of Jesus, every knee, by divine decree, must bow. When Jesus arrives on the scene, light shines. When light arrives, darkness must depart.

The king of Syria has proved that the enemy, the devil, has great respect for our God—even more so than many Christians.

Arresting
the Arrester

This king sent a whole army to surround the city where Elisha was, to arrest just one prophet. The king had a lot of common sense. He must have learned that Elisha was Elijah's servant and that a king once tried to arrest Elijah with two sets of fifty soldiers and their captains and they became ashes. The king of Syria knew that many soldiers couldn't do the job, so he sent chariots, horses and his best soldiers.

In Acts 19:13-16, we have a classic case of the enemy recognizing the name Jesus Christ. The seven sons of Sceva, a Jewish priest, took it upon themselves to cast out demons in the name of Jesus, whom Paul preaches. The devil answered that he knew Jesus. Demons know there is someone called Jesus, and they know they must bow at His name.

A demon-possessed boy was once brought to me for prayer. He could neither walk nor kneel. I commanded him to kneel. He asked me in whose name? I told him in the name of Jesus, and he said that was different, and he knelt. I told him to walk in the name of Jesus, and he again responded that the name was different and instantly obeyed. The demon in him recognized the name of Jesus Christ.

1 Samuel 4:5-7 tells of the Philistines being afraid of the ark of the Lord that was brought into the camp of the children of Israel. Demons shake when they hear about our God.

We, God's children, have to rejoice because we have a great Father. With Him, we are more than conquerors. We shall be on top only. We will never be beneath. There is no weapon fashioned against us that will prosper. Daniel tells of an idol worshipper's perception of our God:

> *Then King Darius wrote to all the peoples, nations and men of every language throughout the land: 'May you prosper greatly! I issue a decree that in every part of my kingdom, people must fear and reverence the God of*

Daniel. For he is the living God, and he endures forever; his kingdom will not be destroyed, his dominion will never end. He rescues and he saves; he performs signs and wonders in the heavens and on the earth. He has rescued Daniel from the power of the lions.'

(Daniel 6:25-27)

When you want somebody to write a testimonial about you, you look to your best friend, who will write good things about you. When an enemy writes a testimonial about his enemy and states that He delivers, and works signs and wonders, you better believe it.

It is also important to note that God can perform many wonders in one single night. A lot can happen in one night. In Judges 16:2, 3, for example, Samson was in Gaza, and the people shut the gates against him with plans to kill him the next morning. At midnight, empowered by the Holy Spirit, he uprooted the gates and dumped them on the mountaintop. Similarly, all the gates that have been shut against you can be uprooted in one night.

In another example, in Acts 16:25, 26, Paul and Silas were in prison. They were special prisoners because they praised God, even in their chains. Suddenly, there was an earthquake, and every yoke was broken. All your yokes can be broken, in the spiritual realm, in one night.

Acts 12:5-10 tells Peter's prison story. The king had decided that the following morning would be his execution day. On the night before, when the enemy was sleeping, an angel woke up Peter to tell him his day of freedom had come. The prison doors opened of their own accord. Just the same, in one night, every door that has been shut on you can open.

In the story of King Sennacherib, the powerful king who had captured many nations and desecrated many gods (2 kings

Arresting the Arrester

19), He decided not only to fight the nation of Israel, but also to insult her God. During the night, God sent only one angel to his camp to kill all his soldiers. One angel of the Lord also can deal with everyone who has been plotting your destruction.

In another example, Daniel spent one night in the lions' den, and God shut the mouth of death. All you need is for God to shut the mouth of death for just one night so you can escape forever. It takes God just one night to straighten out a lot in your life, physically, spiritually and in all aspects of your life. This is why Psalm 30:5 states that

> For his anger lasts only a moment, but his favor lasts a lifetime; weeping may remain for a night, but rejoicing comes in the morning.

May you rejoice as you and the Almighty God together defeat your enemies.

Chapter Six

Trust Only in
the Living God

As you fight spiritual warfares, you will encounter problems along the way. At times you would feel distressed or hopeless or a whole range of emotions that will try to overcome you. It's during these times that you must trust that God will make everything all right in your life, as long as you stay close to Him and serve Him.

Elisha trusted God when the king of Syria sent an army to capture him:

> Then he sent horses and chariots and a strong force there. They went by night and surrounded the city. When the servant of the man of God got up and went out early the next morning, an army with horses and chariots had surrounded the city. 'Oh, my lord, what shall we do?' the

Arresting
the Arrester

servant asked. 'Don't be afraid,' the prophet answered. 'Those who are with us are more than those who are with them'. (2 Kings 6:14-16)

When Elisha's servant woke up in the morning, he knew immediately that they had come to arrest his master. When the servant informed Elisha of this, he was not at all moved. Elisha, a "man of God," told him not to worry because all was well and that those who were with them were more than the enemies.

Also, by saying "the servant of the man of God," it means the man was not just serving an ordinary person, but was serving the Almighty God through the man of God. Anyone who serves the man of God does it for his God and will receive the reward directly from God.

This is stated in Matthew 10:40-42. Jesus said that he who receives His disciples receives Him, and he who receives Him receives He who sent Him. He that receives a prophet in the name of a prophet shall receive a prophet's reward, and he that receives a righteous man in the name of a righteous man shall receive the reward of a righteous man. Anything you do for a man of God, you have done for the God who sent him, and God will reward you.

Learn to Serve

If you want the blessings of a man of God, you must learn to serve. You can't know how to lead until you learn how to follow. Therefore, anyone who wants the anointing of Elijah must first serve Elijah.

In 2 Kings 3:11, the Bible says Elisha was the one who poured water on Elijah's hands. Elisha served Elijah, and this was why he got a double portion of the anointing of Elijah. Anyone who

wants the recognition of God
must be ready to do the work
that Joshua did. Joshua was
the servant of Moses. When
Moses died, God said He would be with Joshua just as He was
with Moses. If you want the blessings of Moses, you must do
the work of Joshua.

On the other hand, any man who attacks a true man of God
will have to answer to God. Psalm 105:14, 15 clearly states
that God permits no one to harm His anointed or His
prophets. This was what God told Saul of Tarsus on his way to
Damascus. God told Paul it was Him Paul was opposing by
harassing Christians.

In the story of the king of Syria, Elisha's servant got up early to
seek God and to serve. Anyone who is an early riser has a lot
of blessings to gain. When you wake up early, particularly as a
child of God, I am sure the first thing you want to do is seek
God, praise Him and rejoice that you are alive. You want to be
like David, who said in Psalm 63:1 that he loved to seek God
early. A true child of God will do this. Those who seek God
early always find Him.

> I love those who love me, and those who seek me find
> me. (Proverbs 8:17)

Besides, anybody who wants to serve God, particularly in
these last days, will have to be in a hurry and be diligent.
Hebrews 11:6 states that God rewards those who diligently
seek Him. If you do not move fast, you cannot work with God
because the end is near, and God is in a hurry. The Almighty
is coming soon, and I advise you to be ready. Your reward from
Him will be according to what you have done already, not
what you plan to do.

Those who wake up early are the ones to hear the first good
news. This happened on the day of resurrection (Matthew

Arresting
the Arrester

28:1-6). Mary, the mother of Jesus, and Mary Magdalene were the first to hear that Jesus had risen.

When the servant of the man of God woke up, he saw a great host surrounding them. We notice that the great host arrived the night before but did not attack throughout the night. This gives us the comfort that though the enemy may gather against you in the night, he will not be allowed to attack you because there is Someone who looks after you who neither slumbers nor sleeps. Regardless of what may be happening in the rest of the world, no evil will come into your house as long as you remain close to Jesus Christ.

The fact that the servant saw a great host when he arose means it will be followed by a great testimony. Testimonies always begin with problems. The bigger the problem, the greater the testimony will be. If you have a big problem now, it means your testimony will be great. When God wants to do something great, He starts with a big problem. When God wants to perform a miracle, He starts with what seems impossible.

In the story of David and Goliath, Goliath was a big problem to David, but God knocked him out with a little stone. In another example, three great kings gathered against Jehoshaphat, but at the end of the day, all the wealth of the three kings came into the treasury of Jehoshaphat. Also, when the Israelites came to the Red Sea and saw Pharaoh in pursuit, it seemed there was no way out, but God performed a miracle.

"Oh!"

In the story of the king of Syria, we can tell there is trouble by one little word. The servant turned to his master, Elisha, and said, "Oh." In this story, "oh" can mean several things. It can be the cry of the helpless, since they had no weapons of warfare. You may be in this situation now. But according to Psalm

46:1-3, God is your refuge and strength and a very present help in the time of trouble.

"Oh" also can be the cry of the distressed and sorrowful. If you are in this state, remember there is Someone who is ready to help the distressed. If you call on Him, He will hear you (Psalm 120:1).

"Oh" can be the cry of the hopeless. If you feel hopeless, you better put all your hope in God, and I can assure you that you will have cause to praise God, just as David did in Psalm 43:5. As long as God is still in you, your case is not hopeless, as Colossians 1:27 says: *"Christ in you, the hope of glory."*

"Oh" also can be the cry of someone who is deeply frightened. If you are in this type of situation, turn your attention to God, and your fears will flee.

> *The Lord is my light and my salvation—whom shall I fear? The Lord is the stronghold of my life—of whom shall I be afraid? When evil men advance against me to devour my flesh, when my enemies and my foes attack me, they will stumble and fall. Though an army besiege me, my heart will not fear; though war break out against me, even then will I be confident.*
> (Psalm 27:1-3)

Finally, "Oh" may be the cry of somebody who is sinking and suffocating with problems. In Psalm 28:1, David said he would cry unto God, his Rock, and that God should not ignore him. Even when God had sentenced Hezekiah to death, he still cried to God. God heard him and prolonged his life. If you find yourself sinking, and you call on God, He will help you. Even in the belly of the fish, Jonah still cried to God (Psalm 130:1-3).

Arresting
the Arrester

Put Your Trust in God

Everyone has someone he or she turns to in times of trouble. When trouble comes, some people turn to the occult, while some turn to secret societies or idols. Some turn to false prophets. 1 Kings 18:26-29 reveals how some people called on Baal, but he did not hear them. My God hears, and He is always available. Do not turn to idols with mouths that cannot speak.

Do not put your trust even in a man of God. Put your trust in God only. Do not tie your faith to a man. The moment you trust in the prayers and powers of a man, you are putting a curse on yourself. If God does not allow that man to pray for you, you will die. As Psalm 125:1-5 states, trust in the Lord and abide forever. Only the Almighty God is available all the time. Idols are useless to themselves and those who serve them, as shown in 1 Samuel 5:2-5. Renounce all those idols, astrologers, tarot card readers, fortunetellers, secret societies, and occult and new age groups because you know they have not helped you. Come to the Living God.

In the above passage, Elisha's servant said, "My lord." He did not just say "Lord." This means that who your helper will be in times of trouble is a personal decision. That is why David said in Psalm 121:1, 2 that he will lift up his eyes unto the hills, from where he gets help. He personalized the statement, as he did in almost all the Psalms he wrote (Psalm 23, Psalm 31).

The servant also asked, "What shall we do?" Once in a while, we find ourselves in a situation where there seems to be no way out. But remember, if you are a true child of God, there is always a way out. God always will make a way where there seems to be no way. If He has to create dry land in the Red Sea, He will do it. He has done it before. If He has to bring water out of the rock, He will do it. He has also done that before. If He has to create a special fish for you, as He did in the case of Jonah, He will do that.

Trust Only in the Living God

Those who trust in God will never be put to shame. When there seems to be no way, turn to the One who is the Way, and He will walk you through even locked doors, as in Peter's case in Acts 12:10.

When you put your trust in the Almighty God, even during troubled times, you have nothing to fear.

Just as Elisha answered his servant immediately when he asked him what they would do, whenever you call on the Almighty God, He does not delay His answers.

God makes this promise in Jeremiah:

> *Call to me and I will answer you and tell you great and unsearchable things you do not know.* (Jeremiah 33:3)

Let Go of Sin

There is only one reason you may call and He will not answer, and that's if there is sin in your life, and you refuse to let go of it. Let go of sin so the power of God can work in and for you.

> *When I called, you answered and made me bold and stout-hearted.* (Psalm 138:3)

This is God's way. God does not delay. He does not enjoy seeing His people in poverty, sickness or sorrow. He does not want you to suffer. If you let go of sin, there is no reason why your prayer will not be answered immediately.

> *Before they call I will answer; while they are still speaking I will hear.* (Isaiah 65:24)

Arresting
the Arrester

Fear Not

Elisha responded immediately to his servant and said, "Don't be afraid," or, "Fear not." There are 365 places in the Bible where we find "fear not." This means there is one "fear not" for every day of the year.

"Fear not" can mean several things. First, it could mean there is something that can cause fear, but the Almighty God is saying you should pay no attention to it. Fear comes through something that you see or hear. 2 Corinthians 5:7 states that we walk by faith and not by sight. In other words, we refuse to look at anything that brings fear. Psalm 112 states that we shall not be afraid of evil tidings:

> *He will have no fear of bad news; his heart is steadfast,*
> *trusting in the Lord. His heart is secure, he will have no*
> *fear; in the end he will look in triumph on his foes.*
>
> (Psalm 112:7, 8)

Faith also comes by what we hear (Romans 10:17). When the others bring their evil reports from the devil, you are to ignore these and hear only the reports from the Lord. You will have to make a choice. The report of God is that with Him, nothing is impossible.

"Fear not" also can mean that things are not what they seem to be. Many a time, we see no way out of our problems, but the view from above shows that there is nothing to fear at all. Some of us are still afraid of the wicked people of the world, even though we know the Bible states that greater is He that is in us than he that is in the world. We are also aware that the Word of God states that we are more than conquerors.

When demons see you, because you are a child of God, they also see the light of God shining in you. They see the seal of ownership of the Almighty God on you. You have to make up

your mind to chase demons
and not to run away from
them.

"Fear not" also can mean that the problem that is frightening you has been taken care of by the only One who is far stronger and more powerful than you are. In John 16:33, Jesus said in this world, we will have tribulations, but we should be of good cheer because He has overcome the world.

God took care of the problem at the Red Sea. When the children of Israel got to the Red Sea and saw Pharaoh's army in hot pursuit, fear overcame them. But Moses allayed their fears when he told them they would never see the enemies again after that moment. God had His aces ready, and He played them when the Red Sea opened up for Israel to pass through on dry land.

The Lord does not want us to be afraid:

> But now, this is what the Lord says—he who created you, O Jacob, he who formed you, O Israel: 'Fear not, for I have redeemed you; I have summoned you by name; you are mine. When you pass through the waters, I will be with you; and when you pass through the rivers, they will not sweep over you. When you walk through the fire, you will not be burned; the flames will not set you ablaze. For I am the Lord, your God, the Holy One of Israel, your Savior; I give Egypt for your ransom, Cush and Seba in your stead.' (Isaiah 43:1-3)

We shouldn't be afraid of what will happen tomorrow. All will be well because God has already taken care of your tomorrow, and He has decided that it is going to be well with you.

Elisha gave his reason for telling his servant not to fear. He said their friends were more than their foes. Who are the "they" boosting Elisha's confidence? I know that God the Father is with us. Psalm 104:32 states that the One who is with us, looks at the earth and it trembles. Psalm 68:1, 2 states that

Arresting
the Arrester

when God arises, His enemies scatter. Jesus Christ never leaves us. Philippians 2:9-11 states that God has given Jesus Christ a name that is above every other name, and that at the mention of the name of Jesus, every knee shall bow.

God the Holy Spirit is also with us. It is God the Holy Spirit that is called the Consuming Fire in Hebrews 12:29. This is why Jesus said if you offend the Father, He will forgive you. Also, if you offend the Son, there is hope for you. However, if you offend the Holy Spirit, there will be trouble for you in this world and in the world to come. That is why your enemy is in trouble if you are on the side of the Lord. If you are against God, you are playing with fire. As a matter of fact, Hebrews 10:31 states that it is a fearful thing to fall into the hands of the living God.

In addition, the angels of heaven are with us. Hebrews 1:13, 14 states that angels are our servants. They are servants of born-again believers. Also, Hebrews 1:7 states that these angels are flames of fire round us.

The Bible states that in Romans 8:31 that if God is for us, nobody can be against us. In Joshua 1:5, God told Joshua that He would be with him as He was with Moses, and no man was ever able to withstand him. As it was true with Joshua, so it is true with us. When God is with you, nobody can stand in your way. When God is with you, your prayers will be answered by fire.

Elisha included his servant in God's divine protection. Elisha did not say, "Those who are with me," he said, "Those who are with us." This means if you follow a true man of God and become associated with someone who is a Holy Ghost carrier, his bodyguards automatically become yours. Those who are taking care of him also will take care of those who belong to him.

This is illustrated in Acts 27:21-24, which tells how Paul was on a ship to Rome as a prisoner, and there was a nasty storm. God told Paul he would not die and that because of him, everyone in the ship would land safely.

When you hook up to a man of God, suddenly, special protection becomes yours. As a matter of fact, if you link up with a man of God, even if you do something that ought to lead to punishment by God, He will ask permission from the man of God to deal with you. There is an example in Exodus 32:9, 10, where God asked Moses to stand aside so He could punish the children of Israel who offended Him. Moses asked for forgiveness, and God spared them.

Be careful who you keep company with. Proverbs 13:20 states that if you walk with the wise, you will become wise. Proverbs 22:24, 25 advises you not to befriend an angry man so as not to get into a trap. Be careful who leads you. If your leader is someone God has forsaken, and you remain with him, when he is going into Hell, I hope you will not go with him.

Strength in Numbers

The good news is our defenders outnumber the enemies. This is what Elisha meant when he said, "Those who are with us are more." According to Revelation 12:3, 4, when the devil fell, he took only one third of the angels of heaven with him. This means that for every demon, there are two angels. If one demon is facing you, you have at least two angels defending you. Daniel needed these angels. Daniel 10:12-14 states that when Daniel prayed, God sent an angel to give him the answer. But a demon stopped the angel on the way, and there was a struggle. After some time, God sent a second angel to go and deal with the demon so the answer could get to Daniel.

Arresting
the Arrester

Our defenders not only have numerical strength, they are also more powerful. 2 Kings 19:32-35 recalls that one angel killed 185,000 soldiers in one night.

So before you begin to think about how big your problem is, maybe you need to think about how big your God is. Is your god the one that can be put inside a pocket or the one whose plans for you can be read from flimsy tarot cards, or is he the one who speaks only through the effigies and Buddhist incantations, or the use of talisman, bracelets and rings? The God I serve is the One in Psalm 91:

He who dwells in the shelter of the Most High will rest in the shadow of the Almighty. (Psalm 91:1)

This means no matter how high the enemy may be, he cannot be as high as the Most High. No matter how powerful your enemy may be, he cannot be more powerful than the Almighty.

No matter how severe your sickness may be, it cannot be as great as the One whose name is the Resurrection and the Life. No matter the storm in your life, it cannot defy the One who is the Prince of Peace. If you are on God's side, you are on the winning side. This was what Elisha implied. The winning side is the shouting side. In 1 Samuel 17:51, 52, the Bible states that the men of Israel and Judah shouted after David slew Goliath because they had won. Many times, you may need to shout to usher in your victory. But you must trust in God, that if He is with you, you will win.

Chapter Seven

God Will
Deliver Again

Why did Elisha trust God when a whole army was sent just for him? Why was he able to remain calm when surrounded by a host of military men and might?

It was simply because he knew a little bit of divine history. His forefathers had told him about the extraordinary exploits of the God he served. He was also aware that his God is an unchangeable God. Elisha was unshaken because he knew the God of his forefathers, the God of Elijah, his spiritual father. He knew without any doubt that he was serving a God who repeats miracles.

We are serving a God who can duplicate miracles. If God has performed a miracle before, He can repeat it. Surely, Elisha was there when a king sent fifty soldiers and a captain to arrest Elijah (2 Kings 1:9-12). When the soldiers got to Elijah, he

Arresting
the Arrester

verified his status as a man of God by commanding fire from heaven on the soldiers.

Before Elijah finished speaking, the captain and his fifty soldiers had become ashes. The king sent another set of fifty soldiers and a captain, and God repeated the miracle through Elijah. The God who had earlier answered the prayer of Elijah by fire on Mount Carmel (1 Kings 18) can do it again.

Elisha was also aware that on the last journey of Elijah, when both of them got to the Jordan River, Elijah smote the river with his mantle, and the water parted for them to walk on dry ground. After Elijah was taken to heaven and Elisha had taken over his mantle, God performed the miracle again for Elisha to pass over the Jordan.

He'll Do It Again!

The beauty of this miracle is that before the Lord parted the Jordan River for Elijah and Elisha, He had done it for Joshua. This assures us that what God has done before for others, He can do for us. If God can open one blind eye, He can open yours, too. If He had healed deafness in one person, there is no reason why He cannot heal your ears, too. If He had made just one lame to walk, there is no reason you should not walk. If He had paid one person's debt, you can regard your own debt as already paid. If He can make one infertile woman conceive, it is certain that your conception will not be impossible with God. God is no respecter of persons. As a matter of fact, that's why we give testimonies, because faith comes by hearing, and hearing by the Word of God.

Elisha knew from experience that the God of his father is a great Deliverer and that having delivered before, He can deliver again. David believed this as well.

The Lord who delivered me from the paw of the lion and the paw of the bear will deliver me from the hand of this Philistine.
(1 Samuel 17:37)

When Shadrach, Meshach and Abednego were brought before king Nebuchadnezzar, and he asked them to bow to his idol or they would be put in the fiery furnace, the three Hebrew children said the God whom they served was able to deliver and that He would deliver them.

You need to know that the God you serve is able to deliver you, too, and He will. He is able to heal you, and He will. He is able to answer your prayers, and He will.

Why were Shadrach, Meshach and Abednego so sure that God would deliver them from the fiery furnace? It's simple: Like Elisha and David, they knew He had done it before. He had delivered them and Daniel from king Nebuchadnezzar's order to kill all wise men when he needed his dream interpreted (Daniel 2). The plan of the devil was that they would die. Instead, they were promoted. The same God delivered Daniel from the den of lions.

Elisha—Unshaken

Elisha was unshaken and unshakable because he knew his God. In Philippians 3:7-10, Paul states that there is no cost too high to pay to know God. Daniel tells what will happen to those who know their God:

With flattery he will corrupt those who have violated the covenant, but the people who know their God will firmly resist him. (Daniel 11:32)

Arresting
the Arrester

While others are confused, those who know their God will be calm. Not only will they be strong, they will do exploits as well. You must know Him, too, so you can perform feats.

Not only did Elisha know God, but he knew God had a purpose for his life and that the purpose was yet to be fully accomplished. He knew he couldn't possibly die when God's purpose was not yet fulfilled. God has a purpose for your life, and you cannot die until that purpose is fulfilled. Until God finishes with you, nobody can kill you.

But have you discovered God's purpose for your life? Anyone who discovers God's purpose for his or her life will never go astray but will follow that purpose. At the end of the day, he or she will look back and give glory to God. After all, you were created for the pleasure of the Almighty God (Revelation 4:10, 11). If you have not given God much of the pleasure for which you were pre-ordained, then you cannot die yet. It is not over until God says it is over.

Unlike Elisha, his servant was worried. That's because Elisha could see what his servant could not see. His servant had ordinary eyes, while Elisha had extra perception. He was able to tell the servant that their friends were superior and numerically stronger. Believe it or not, those who are on your side are more than your enemies.

When it comes to knowing God, there are degrees of knowledge. There is a difference between hearing about God and seeing God. Elisha's servant did not see anything apart from the two of them. Elisha saw something extra, which made him confident. It is a good thing to see what ordinary eyes cannot. However, Jesus told Thomas in John 20:29, "Blessed are those who have not seen and yet have believed. Then in turn, according to John 11:40, if you believe, you will see the glory of God.

You may not be able to see angels, but when you believe without seeing, you bring pleasure to God. Everything is possible to those who believe. When you have faith, you please God. Without faith, it is impossible to please God. You may not be able to see like Elisha, but you can exercise faith.

It is also important to get to know Jesus before trouble comes calling on you. Elisha did not begin to search for God on the day of trouble. However, many people search for God only when trouble comes. This is a bad idea. If God is not in your boat before the storm comes, how will He calm the storm? Seek the Lord when He may be found so He can rebuke the storms in your life.

Then keep the relationship going. Elisha was not an occasional visitor to God. You need divine nourishment to keep you going day by day. Morning and afternoon prayer, Bible studies and house fellowship meetings are good links to God.

A resident, not a visitor, is the only one who can say he or she is under the shadow of the Almighty (Psalm 91:1). In addition, those who are connected to God every day develop a strong trust in God and they are the kind of people nothing can move.

Chapter Eight

the Gift of the

Discerning of

Spirits

One of the miracles God performs repeatedly is giving the gift of the discerning of spirits. It's a gift that He keeps on giving.

Elisha's servant received this gift:

> *And Elisha prayed, 'O Lord, open his eyes so he may see.' Then the Lord opened the servant's eyes, and he looked and saw the hills full of horses and chariots of fire all around Elisha.* (2 Kings 6:17)

The young man could not understand his master, so Elisha prayed to God to open his spiritual eyes that he may see. Immediately, Elisha prayed, God heard, and He answered. God can answer your prayer the moment you pray.

God opened the eyes of the servant of Elisha, and he saw things that ordinary eyes could not see. There are so many

Arresting
the Arrester

things that ordinary eyes cannot see–and they are even more powerful than those things that we can see. For example, we cannot see the air we breathe, but it is more powerful than the water we see. Electricity is another example.

The Word of God is very powerful, yet we cannot see it. Also, we cannot see the anointing, the power of God that breaks the yoke, yet it is awesome. Hebrews 11:3 states that the things that are seen are made by the things that are not seen. Psalm 107:20 states that God sent His word and He healed them and delivered them from their destruction. The invisible is there.

The fact that the servant's spiritual eyes were opened is a gift from God. When you are baptized in the Holy Spirit, the Holy Spirit can give you certain gifts. There are nine of them, recorded in 1 Corinthians 12:4-10. The gift of the discerning of spirits is one of them. If you have it, you can differentiate between angels and demons. To do this, you should be able to see them and hear them speak. (Note that this gift is not the same as the gift of discernment or the gift of suspicion, which are not from the Holy Spirit, but from the devil.)

The Gift of Discerning of Spirits

Why does God give the gift of the discerning of spirits?

(1) God gives this gift particularly when He wants you to know the purpose for your life. There is an example in Exodus 3:1-10, when God revealed His purpose to Moses by opening His spiritual eyes, and he saw a bush burning and the bush was not consumed. The fire that he saw was the fire of God. Ordinary eyes could not see it. God talked to Him and told him the purpose for his life.

Similarly, in Judges 6:11-16, Gideon's spiritual eyes were opened, and he saw an angel who told him God's purpose for his life.

the Gift of the Discerning of Spirits

In Isaiah 6:1-8, God opened the eyes of Isaiah, and he heard God's commission. It is only God who can clearly tell you His purpose for your life because He made the plan. Many a time, God will not let somebody else know about His plan for your life.

(2) God can grant you this gift to assist you in spiritual warfare. If you are a true child of God, the battle line is drawn between you and the devil. In Joshua 5:13-6:5, Joshua was given the gift of the discerning of spirits so he could receive divine assistance in the war against Jericho. God opened his eyes, and he saw a man who was really an angel of God. The angel gave him the strategy for success in the battle against Jericho. This gift is necessary for a spiritual warrior.

(3) God can give you this gift when He wants to give you specific instructions, especially when He wants to do certain things in your life. One example is in Judges 13:2-5, when God sent an angel to Samson's mother to tell her what not to do because she would conceive and give birth to a special child. Another example is found in Acts 10:1-6, which is the story of Cornelius. God decided to save him, so he sent an angel to tell him to send for Peter, who will tell him what to do to be saved.

(4) From time to time, a spiritual warrior may find himself in a storm, desperately needing the presence of God with him. In a situation like this, God will grant him this rare gift, and an angel will allay his fears and assure him that all will be well. An example of this is found in Acts 27:20-25, when prisoner Paul was in a terrible storm. Paul seemed to have lost hope. God sent an angel to tell him he would not die and that he will get to Rome.

(5) Whenever somebody who is faithful to God is in a critical situation, God will open his eyes so he will see either an angel or God Himself keeping him company. When Shadrach,

Arresting
the Arrester

Meshach and Abednego were thrown into the fiery furnace because they refused to bow to idols (Daniel 3:23-25), God Himself joined them there. He opened their eyes, and they saw Him. Also, when Daniel was thrown into the lions' den (Daniel 6), God sent an angel, who shut the mouths of the lions.

(6) God gives this gift to help pilgrims on the path of righteousness. When God finds out you need extra help, particularly when He has a big assignment for you, He will open your eyes and ears, and you will see and hear heavenly things and hear heavenly discussions. A good example is found in 2 Corinthians 12:1-4, where Paul was taken to the heavens, and God showed him the beauty there. He allowed him to hear certain things. When he came back, he said nothing could separate him from the love of God.

(7) God may give you the gift of the discerning of spirits to let you know the roots of your problems. In other words, He may open your eyes to see what is preventing your progress. There is a good example in the story of Balaam, who was bent on bending the barometer of God's will (Numbers 23:21-26). So an angel stood in his way. The donkey on which he was riding saw the angel and tried to avoid him. But Balaam saw nothing. God had to open his eyes to see the angel standing ready to destroy him.

(8) God may grant you this gift to bless you, particularly if you are a prayer warrior. Genesis 32:24-28 illustrates this well. As Jacob made his way back from many years of serving his uncle Laban, a man wrestled with him at night. Jacob was to meet Esau the next day. Esau had promised to kill Jacob, so he needed a miracle immediately. After the wrestling bout, Jacob asked for a special blessing, and the angel blessed him. This was why God sent the angel.

(9) From time to time, God wants to reward His faithful friends, and He sends an angel to bring them blessings or just

to open their eyes to new knowledge. When God wanted to fulfill His promise to Abraham, He visited him. When Moses wanted to see the glory of God, God showed him. Also, Elisha asked Elijah for a double portion of his anointing (2 Kings 2:9-11). Elijah said the request was difficult, but that if Elisha saw him when he was being taken away, he would get what he requested. God opened the eyes of Elisha because he had been a faithful servant.

(10) When a spiritual warrior finds himself in a difficult situation, God will send an angel to get him out. In Acts 12:5-11, Peter was in prison, and an angel came to rescue him.

(11) When God wants to send you a special message, He sends angels. In Luke 1:26-38, an angel told Mary that she would give birth to a baby to be named Jesus. Mary wondered how this could be possible since she was a virgin and not yet married, and the angel told her that the Holy Spirit would overshadow her. Another example is in Luke 1:11-17. When God revealed to Zacharias that he would have a son, God opened his spiritual eyes to see the angel that brought the good news. Also, in Revelation 1:10-12, when God wanted to reveal to John the divine truths about the last days, He opened his spiritual eyes to see the things that would happen.

(12) When God wants to share especially good news with just a few people, He sends angels. Luke 2:8-14 states that while shepherds watched their flock by night, an angel appeared and gave them the good news that the Savior had been born.

The Seven Fortified Walls

Like when God opened the eyes of Elisha's servant, God uses this gift to allay our fears by showing us we are safe. Whether we see it or not, every child of God has a security system made of seven walls that no enemy can penetrate. Sometimes God

Arresting
the Arrester

gives us the gift of the discerning of spirits so we can see we are safe.

(1) The wall of the blood of Jesus. The day you became born again, you were washed in the blood of Jesus Christ. Not only does the blood cleanse you from all sins, it also builds a wall of protection around every child of God. Before any demon gets to anyone with this protection, it would have to figure out how to cross the bloodline.

(2) The wall of fire. There is a wall of fire around you as a child of God. You may not see it, but it is there. If anyone tries to harm you, they will be consumed by fire. This is illustrated in Zechariah:

> *'And I myself will be a wall of fire around it,' declares the Lord, 'and I will be its glory within.'* (Zechariah 2:5)

(3) The wall of angels. The angel of the Lord makes his camp around you to protect you.

> *The angel of the Lord encamps around those who fear him, and he delivers them.* (Psalm 34:7)

One angel, according to 2 Kings 19:35, can destroy 185,000 soldiers in one night. I don't think you have that many enemies.

(4) The wall of His name.

> *The name of the Lord is a strong tower; the righteous run to it and are safe.* (Proverbs 18:10)

If you have the name of Jesus Christ and you are still afraid, it may mean that you are not born again. If you are truly born again, you have the right to use the name of Jesus. At the name of Jesus Christ, every knee must bow.

(5) The wall of His shadows.

He who dwells in the shelter of the Most High will rest in the shadow of the Almighty. (Psalm 91:1)

When you are living under the shadow of the Almighty, nobody can touch you, and there is nothing to fear day or night because the One keeping you will neither sleep nor slumber (Psalm 121:3-5).

(6) **The wall of His wings.** God covers His own like a mother hen covers her chicks from the attack of an eagle. When His wings cover you, no evil can reach you.

He will cover you with his feathers, and under his wings you will find refuge; his faithfulness will be your shield and rampart. (Psalm 91:4)

(7) **The wall of His presence.**

Those who trust in the Lord are like Mount Zion, which cannot be shaken but endures forever. As the mountains surround Jerusalem, so the Lord surrounds his people both now and forevermore. The scepter of the wicked will not remain over the land allotted to the righteous, for then the righteous might use their hands to do evil. (Psalm 125:1-3)

As mountains surround Jerusalem, so the Lord surrounds His children. Anyone who wants to come in has to pass through Jesus Christ. Fire could not burn Shadrach, Meshach and Abednego in the furnace because the Lord was with them.

These solid walls surround the children of God. They are, however, useless if you do not stay within them. The Bible contains several examples of staying within God's walls of protection. In Exodus 12:22, God told the children of Israel to mark their door posts with blood and that no one should go

Arresting
the Arrester

out until morning. In Joshua 2:12-19, the spies Joshua sent told Rehab to tie a red string on her window and anyone within her house shall be safe. Psalm 91:1 states that you have to dwell in the secret place of the Most High, not be a visitor. Proverbs 18:10 advises you to run into the strong tower to be saved.

If you are not yet born again, make up your mind today that you will run to Jesus so you can be surrounded by these walls and stay within them. If you are born again, ask God to seal the cracks in the walls of your life.

Chapter Nine

Your Enemy

is Under

your Feet

How will you deal with battles? You have five options:

(1) Pretend you have no enemies. If you think like this, you must be a fool because 1 Peter 5:8 expects you to:

> Be self-controlled and alert. Your enemy the devil prowls around like a roaring lion looking for someone to devour.

You have at least one enemy, and his name is Satan. However, he is your number two enemy. Your number one enemy is yourself–your flesh that will ask you to do what God says you should not do. Satan does not work alone. He has an army of supporters, according to Ephesians 6:12. He has principalities, powers, rulers of darkness and all kinds of demons supporting him to steal your joy, to kill, to destroy the life of God that you

Arresting
the Arrester

live. To pretend you have no enemy is utter foolishness (John 10:10).

(2) Run from battles. How long are you going to run? Many of us have been running for years. You are afraid of your roots and only visit your family with trepidation. Haters of God and doers of iniquity are just a few in the dense demography of darkness, which covers the whole earth (Isaiah 60:2). How far will you run? If you run, you are done. Christians must never run from battles.

(3) Get somebody else to fight for you. In the past, many people have consulted occult powers, mingled with magic and courted fortune cards, crystal balls or contrary spirits. It is a dangerous thing to let someone else fight your battle for you, while you are hiding. Jeremiah 17:5, 6 reminds us that cursed is the one who puts his trust in man. Those who invite you to consult them lead you away from your victory.

(4) Face your battles squarely. When you fight it out yourself, you develop your spiritual muscles. You will pray and pray hard, but remember that prayers do not change God. God does not change (Malachi 3:6). Jesus does not change (Hebrews 13:8). This should not discourage you from praying. As a matter of fact, you have to pray without ceasing, according to the Bible.

The problem with fighting battles yourself is that with your human frailties, sooner or later, you will get tired. Exodus 17:11, 12 states that when Moses would raise his hands up, the children of Israel would prevail over the Amalekites. But whenever he lowered his hands, the Amalekites prevailed. As Moses got tired of raising his hands, as he reached his limits, at one time or another, you will reach your limits as a human being. We should keep fasting so we can become razor sharp for the Lord. We must keep praying so our spiritual muscles will remain fully developed.

Even youths grow tired and weary, and young men stumble and fall.
(Isaiah 40:30)

Even if you are young and full of strength, sooner or later, you will peak and plateau at some point on your endurance trail. At times, so many problems hit you so fast that you may not know how to pray.

(5) Let God fight your battles for you while you praise Him.

But those who hope in the Lord will renew their strength. They will soar on wings like eagles; they will run and not grow weary, they will walk and not be faint.
(Isaiah 40:31)

The only way to victory is to let God fight your battles for you—just as He did for the Israelites in the Red Sea; for Shadrach, Meshach and Abednego in the fiery furnace; and for Daniel in the lions' den. Don't fight for yourselves.

The Lord will fight for you; you need only to be still.
(Exodus 14:14)

Resist the Enemy

You must stand and face your enemies with God, and not turn from them.

When the enemies came against Elisha, he did not run. Instead, as the host that surrounded Elisha and his servant closed in on them, Elisha prayed that God would bind them with blindness. As soon as Elisha finished praying, God answered. He blinded them or dulled their minds, making them zombies.

Arresting
the Arrester

As the enemy came down toward him, Elisha prayed to the Lord, 'Strike these people with blindness.' So he struck them with blindness, as Elisha had asked.

(2 Kings 6:18)

You, too, should stop running from your enemies. God does not expect any of His children to run from the enemy. He does expect you to stand and fight, and He will be right by your side fighting with you.

Finally, be strong in the Lord and in his mighty power. Put on the full armor of God so that you can take your stand against the devil's schemes. For our struggle is not against flesh and blood, but against the rulers, against the authorities, against the powers of this dark world and against the spiritual forces of evil in the heavenly realms. (Ephesians 6:10-12)

If you run, the enemy will chase you. Besides, if you run, God has no armor for your back. Ephesians 6:14-17 makes it clear that God has helmets for our heads, shields for our chests, belts for our waists and shoes for our feet, while the back is not protected.

You are to resist the enemy whenever he comes against you. When you do, he will flee from you.

Submit yourselves, then, to God. Resist the devil, and he will flee from you. (James 4:7)

The devil will always want to try you out for size to see whether you will run from him. If you keep running, he will keep chasing you. The moment you stop running, he will be surprised and eagerly test you to find out how serious you are. So be warned:

68

Be self-controlled and alert. Your enemy the devil prowls around like a roaring lion looking for someone to devour. Resist him, standing firm in the faith, because you know that your brothers throughout the world are undergoing the same kind of sufferings.
(1 Peter 5:8, 9)

You are to resist the devil steadfastly in the faith.

Not only did Elisha refuse to run, he went on the offensive. This is what God expects you to do. You must not wait until the enemy gets the better of you before you act. If the enemy already has gained access, you don't have to wait until he unleashes mayhem before you do something about it. Go on the offensive as soon as you know the enemy is around.

'No weapon forged against you will prevail, and you will refute every tongue that accuses you. This is the heritage of the servants of the Lord, and this is their vindication from me.' (Isaiah 54:17)

This Word of God is forever settled. God says our defense is sure. This defense is impregnable, so we are supposed to be aggressive.

This Proverb assures our safety:

The name of the Lord is a strong tower; the righteous run to it and are safe. (Proverbs 18:10)

Take an Offensive Stance

As many of us who already have run into Jesus Christ, God expects us to move forward and cause every knee to bow at the name of Jesus Christ. David moved forward:

Arresting the Arrester

As the Philistine moved closer to attack him, David ran quickly toward the battle line to meet him. Reaching into his bag and taking out a stone, he slung it and struck the Philistine on the forehead. The stone sank into his forehead, and he fell facedown on the ground. (1 Samuel 17:48, 49)

David made the first move. Do not wait for the enemy to hit you first; hit the enemy first. Every true child of God must be a terror to the devil and his agents. You must learn to take an offensive stance. If you don't get rid of the agents of the devil in your life, they are likely to get rid of you.

As you face your enemies aggressively, it will help to know how to pray effectively, as Elisha prayed to the Lord. The moment the devil knows you do not know what to do when you pray, he will see you as an easy prey.

For prayers to be answered, they must be rendered the way God wants them. When you pray, it must be directed toward God the Father. Whatever your requests, you must ask God the Father, according to Jesus Christ:

> *In that day you will no longer ask me anything. I tell you the truth, my Father will give you whatever you ask in my name.* (John 16:23)

Your request must be in the name of God the Son. If you want to pray but don't know how to pray correctly, ask the Holy Spirit to help you. Consider this:

> *In the same way, the Spirit helps us in our weakness. We do not know what we ought to pray for, but the Spirit himself intercedes for us with groans that words cannot express.* (Romans 8:26)

Praying correctly is like maintaining your car correctly. For your car to perform perfectly, you need oil, water for the radiator and gasoline for the gas tank. If you mix oil, gasoline and water and put it in your engine, it will knock. Likewise, if you do not pray correctly, your prayer may not be answered.

Matthew offers this advice on praying:

> And when you pray, do not keep on babbling like pagans, for they think they will be heard because of their many words. (Matthew 6:7)

The Bible states that there are all kinds of prayers.

> And pray in the Spirit on all occasions with all kinds of prayers and requests. With this in mind, be alert and always keep on praying for all the saints.
>
> (Ephesians 6:18)

There is the prayer of thanksgiving, the prayer of praise, the prayer of supplication and so on. Elisha prayed the prayer of command. He asked God to hit the host of Syrian hitmen with blindness. Can anybody command God? The answer to this question can be deduced from Isaiah:

> This is what the Lord says–the Holy One of Israel, and its Maker: Ask me of things to come concerning my sons and concerning the work of my hands command ye me.
>
> (Isaiah 45:11 King James Version)

It is the Almighty God who gave the great privilege that on certain occasions, subject to certain conditions that we shall see later, we can command Him to do certain things for us, and He will honor us.

Arresting
the Arrester

After all, Matthew implies that whatever you allow on earth will be allowed in heaven:

> *I tell you the truth, whatever you bind on earth will be bound in heaven and whatever you loose on earth will be loosed in heaven.* (Matthew 18:18)

The Conditions for Results

The conditions we have to fulfill before we can say the prayer of command are listed in Job:

> *Submit to God and be at peace with him; in this way prosperity will come to you. Accept instruction from his mouth and lay up his words in your heart. If you return to the Almighty, you will be restored: If you remove wickedness far from your tent and assign your nuggets to the dust, your gold of Ophir to the rocks in the ravines, then the Almighty will be your gold, the choicest silver for you. Surely then you will find delight in the Almighty and will lift up your face to God. You will pray to him, and he will hear you, and you will fulfill your vows. What you decide on will be done, and light will shine on your ways.* (Job 22:21-28)

Here's what you need to do:

(1) Submit to God. You must get to know God. Draw close to the Almighty. Learn about His ways of doing things. Do not base your faith on human wisdom.

(2) Accept His instructions. Let the Word of God be your law. Do whatever the Bible asks of you, and avoid whatever the Bible says to avoid.

(3) Lay up His words in your heart. Memorize the Bible. It is when you know the Bible intimately that you will know what God wants and what He doesn't want.

(4) Return to the Almighty God. Many have drifted from Him. Many of us have fallen asleep, spiritually. Many of us are dozing, spiritually. Let us return to the Almighty God.

(5) Put away iniquity. This means you must not sin. Don't allow sin into your home. Some parents claim to be Christians, yet they allow their children to fornicate under their roof. If you allow sin in your house, You cannot command God and expect Him to honor you. You are the light of the world. You also must be the light in your house. Your children must know that in your house, Holiness rules, and nothing else is acceptable.

(6) Delight in the Lord. Let what you enjoy be centered on the Almighty God. This includes the type of music you listen to and the kind of conversation you enjoy.

(7) Fulfill your vows. God regards those who do not pay their vows as fools.

It is a pleasant thing for someone to be able to live in the awareness that he or she can command and get results immediately. In the prayer of command, you must be specific. You must tell God exactly what you want done because whatever you say will happen. 1 Corinthians 14:8 puts this in perspective: *"Again, if the trumpet does not sound a clear call, who will get ready for battle?"*

You must believe and not doubt that your prayers will be done.

> I tell you the truth, if anyone says to this mountain, 'Go, throw yourself into the sea,' and does not doubt in his heart but believes that what he says will happen, it will be done for him. (Mark 11:23)

73

Arresting
the Arrester

If you do your part, whatever you ask the Father to do for you, He will do, anywhere, anytime. He will always be there to respond.

You did not choose me, but I chose you and appointed you to go and bear fruit–fruit that will last. Then the Father will give you whatever you ask in my name.
(John 15:16)

This means when we pray to God to help us defeat our enemies, God will fight for us.

What is the Lord's response to Elisha's prayer? God smote the enemies with blindness, according to the words of Elisha. This passage in the Bible is enough to convince anyone beyond all reasonable doubt that the Almighty God is a warrior.

The Lord of Hosts

If that isn't enough, Exodus states it plainly:

The Lord is a warrior; the Lord is his name.
(Exodus 15:3)

Our God is a Warrior. Jesus Christ is not a civilian. As a matter of fact, He is the Captain of the hosts of heaven.

This is further illustrated in Psalm 24:

Lift up your heads, O you gates; be lifted up, you ancient doors, that the King of glory may come in. Who is this King of glory? The Lord strong and mighty, the Lord mighty in battle. Lift up your heads, O you gates; lift them up, you ancient doors, that the King of glory may come in. Who is he, this King of glory? The Lord Almighty–he is the King of glory. (Psalm 24:7-10)

Given this, how can a true Christian live in fear? How can my Father be the Lord of hosts, while I live in fear? In the Bible, David didn't.

> *The Lord is my light and my salvation—whom shall I fear? The Lord is the stronghold of my life—of whom shall I be afraid? When evil men advance against me to devour my flesh, when my enemies and my foes attack me, they will stumble and fall. Though an army besiege me, my heart will not fear; though war break out against me, even then will I be confident.* (Psalm 27:1-3)

If the Lord of hosts is your Father, you have nothing to worry about. One of His soldiers, according to 2 Kings 19:35, can kill 185,000 soldiers in one night. Can you imagine what would happen if He were to give you just ten of them? Exodus 14:14 states that the Lord shall fight for you, and you will hold your peace. He is willing to fight your battles if you allow Him to fight. All He expects from you is to tell Him you need His assistance.

> *The Amalekites came and attacked the Israelites at Rephidim. Moses said to Joshua, 'Choose some of our men and go out to fight the Amalekites. Tomorrow I will stand on top of the hill with the staff of God in my hands.' So Joshua fought the Amalekites as Moses had ordered, and Moses, Aaron and Hur went to the top of the hill. As long as Moses held up his hands, the Israelites were winning, but whenever he lowered his hands, the Amalekites were winning. When Moses' hands grew tired, they took a stone and put it under him and he sat on it. Aaron and Hur held his hands up—one on one side, one on the other—so that his hands remained steady till*

75

Arresting
the Arrester

*sunset. So Joshua over-
came the Amalekite army
with the sword.*

(Exodus 17:8-13)

When we lift up our hands to the Lord, we are asking Him to fight for us. As long as those hands are up, our enemies are in trouble. However, your hands have to be clean. If you have not given your life to Jesus Christ, you must surrender to Him now so His blood can cleanse you from all your sins. Then you, too, can lift your hands to him in holiness. And as you do so, you will receive miracles upon miracles, as the Lord fights for you.

Methods of Warfare

God fights in various ways. Below are ten of them. At least one of them will work against your enemy.

(1) Striking the enemy with blindness. Genesis 19:1-11 tells the story of the angelic visit to Lot in Sodom. When the angels got there, Lot invited them into his house. The men of Sodom were so perverse that they wanted to have sex with the angels. Lot offered them his virgin daughters instead, yet they refused. The angels dragged Lot back into the house and then struck the men of Sodom with blindness.

(2) Drowning the enemy: Exodus 14:27, 28 talks about Pharaoh chasing the children of Israel. They came to the Red Sea, and God performed a miracle. God gathered Pharaoh's army and drowned them in the Red Sea. When you suddenly see your enemies gathering, it is not the time to be afraid. It may be that the Lord is gathering them for destruction so as to give you victory.

(3) Burying the enemy alive. Numbers 16 tells the story of the rebellion of Korah, Dathan and Abiram against Moses. Moses reported them to God, and God told him to separate those who supported the opposition from those on the Lord's side. The ground opened up and swallowed those on the side of the enemies, according to the proclamation of Moses.

(4) Throwing bombs. The Almighty God was the first to throw a bomb. Joshua 10:11 tells the story of how five kings came against Joshua. He fought back until the five kings beat a fast retreat with their soldiers. Then God rained bombs of hail on them.

(5) Using the weapon of the enemy to destroy the enemy. This is clear in 1 Samuel 17:50, 51. When David knocked down Goliath with a stone, there was no sword in his hands. To kill the enemy, David used Goliath's sword to cut off his head.

(6) Roasting the enemies. A good example is in 2 Kings 1:9-12. Elijah was on the mountain, and a king sent a captain and his fifty soldiers to arrest him. Elijah responded by calling fire from above to roast them. Another set of soldiers was sent, and the same fate befell them. We are serving a God who answers by fire.

(7) Making the enemies mad. He did this to Nebuchadnezzar in Daniel 4:32 and to king Saul in 1 Samuel 16:14. When a man decides to put himself in the position of God, God has a way of teaching such a man a lesson. He can turn a king into an animal.

(8) By throwing the enemy into the pit he prepared for you. Such was the case in Esther 7:10. A man named Haman's hatred for another man, Mordecai, produced the highest gallows of their time on which Haman planned to execute Mordecai. But Mordecai found favor with God and his Son-in-law, the king. God made the king hate Haman, and he was executed on the same gallows he raised to kill Mordecai.

Arresting
the Arrester

(9) Uprooting the enemy violently. Acts 5:1-11 records what happened to the only two Christians who allowed demons of deception to use them. Ananias and his wife, Saphirra. God could not allow them to contaminate the new move and work of the Holy Spirit in the early church, so He killed both of them on the same day, and they were buried in the same grave.

(10) Paralyzing the enemy. He allows the enemy's eyes to remain open, but he will not be able to do anything. In this way, they will continue to see the glory of God but will remain handicapped. In Psalm 23:5, David said, "You prepare a table before me in the presence of my enemies."

The psalmist confirms God's power to overcome the enemy:

> *May God arise, may his enemies be scattered; may his foes flee before him.* (Psalm 68:1)

The enemies scatter when they discover, as Hebrews 10:31 states, that it is a fearful thing to fall into the hands of the Almighty God.

If you stand firm and face your enemies with the help of the Lord, your enemies will scatter or be defeated. If you know you do not have the right relationship with God, I advise you to get it right with Him not only so he can help you win, but also so He will not deal with you like an enemy.

Chapter Ten

How to **Arrest**

Your **Enemy**

Now you know what you need to do to defeat your enemy. But how do you do it?

When problems come your way, you must divert your enemies away from you and toward Jesus.

After the enemies were struck with blindness in 2 Kings 6:18, they did not recognize Elisha, as they asked him for a prophet named Elisha. When they asked him, he told them they had missed their way:

> *Elisha told them, 'This is not the road and this is not the city. Follow me, and I will lead you to the man you are looking for.' And he led them to Samaria.* (2 Kings 6:19)

Some people may think Elisha lied. I struggled with this act by a man of God until God opened my spiritual eyes. The Lord

Arresting the Arrester

told me Elisha did not lie. The Lord said if sickness came to my house, what would I tell sickness? I said I would tell sickness that it has the wrong house. In my life, sickness must always have the wrong track. Just the same, poverty and the devil are always backing up the wrong road. The same goes for sorrow and everything opposed to God's will for my life. If you are a true child of God, the moment you tell evil it has the wrong person or has taken the wrong route, evil will go somewhere else.

The Response to Sickness

Sickness seems to be the greatest problem of all. If sickness comes knocking at your door, tell sickness that according to 1 Corinthians 6:19, you are the temple of the Holy Spirit. The Holy Spirit lives in you, and wherever the Holy Spirit lives, there is no room for sickness. Romans 8:11 reveals that if the Spirit of the One who raised Jesus Christ from the dead is in you, that same Spirit will give life to your mortal body. So your body should be full of life and vitality.

Matthew 8:1-3 tells the story of a leper. This is an incurable disease, but he refused to accept the verdict of the world. He went to Jesus, knelt, worshipped Him and said if Jesus was willing, he could be healed. Naturally, Jesus was willing to heal him. This case clearly shows that the man told sickness that it had the wrong road. There were many lepers in those days who died lepers because they accepted their life of leprosy. Many people regard sickness as their friend. For instance, many people describe sickness as theirs, i.e. "my sickness," "my backache," "my cold" and so on. By personalizing this evil, they have already accepted sickness, and it will stay with them.

The Response to Demons

Should demons come knocking at your door, will you welcome them? Jesus said in Matthew 5:14 that you are the light of this world. In Genesis 1:4, God called light out of darkness, deliberately keeping them apart. Amos 3:3 questions the compatibility of two people from opposing kingdoms. Are you in agreement with demons? Many spiritually clean people become demon-possessed because somebody suggested that they may be demon-possessed, and they agreed. The moment they agreed, demons took them over.

> *You, dear children, are from God and have overcome them, because the one who is in you is greater than the one who is in the world.* (1 John 4:4)

Many people treat serious issues such as this lightly. They say that they think they have been demon-possessed. They probably have not read the story in Matthew 8:28-32. Jesus Christ got to the city of the Gergesenes. He met a madman who had battalions of demons in him. As soon as he saw Jesus, he knew he was going to be free. There were some pigs around the coastal area nearby, and the demons begged Jesus to let them possess the pigs. The pigs, in turn, decided to die rather than remain demon-possessed, so they ran into the sea and drowned themselves. We have better senses than pigs. Tell the demon in you that it has the wrong guy, and get delivered.

The Response to Sorrow

Should sorrow come knocking at your door, this is how you should answer:

> *You have made known to me the path of life; you will fill me with joy in your presence, with eternal pleasures at your right hand.* (Psalm 16:11)

Arresting
the Arrester

What kind of home is yours? Is it the house of the devil? My house is that of joy because it is the house of God. Tell sorrow that your Commander-in-Chief has commissioned you in 1 Thessalonians 5:16 to rejoice *always*.

David shows a good example in 1 Samuel 30:1-20. He went to war with his men, and when they came back, they discovered that while they were gone, enemies had carted their children, wives and property away. They wept until there were no more tears to shed. All of a sudden, David rejected sorrow. God told David to go after the enemy, and he became victorious, recovering all the loot plus more.

The Response to Death

If death comes knocking at your door, what will you say? You have to tell death that it has no business with you. That is because John 11 states this:

> *Jesus said to her, 'I am the resurrection and the life. He who believes in me will live, even though he dies.*
> (John 11:25)

> *I will not die but live, and will proclaim what the Lord has done.* (Psalm 118:17)

Defeating death is illustrated in 2 Kings 4:18-37 with the story of the Shunamite woman. God gave her a son, but when the child grew, all of a sudden, the child died. The woman told death that it had backed up the wrong road. The woman laid her dead boy on the bed of the man of God in her home but told the man of God in the field that everything was all right. Death was compelled to cough up the child.

The Response to Failure

Should failure come calling, what would be your response? You must tell failure it has missed its way.

> The Lord will make you the head, not the tail. If you pay attention to the commands of the Lord your God that I give you this day and carefully follow them, you will always be at the top, never at the bottom.
>
> (Deuteronomy 28:13)

Since God has ordained me as the head all the time, if failure comes to my house, I will show it to the door because it has the wrong house. The psalmist denies failure:

> The lions may grow weak and hungry, but those who seek the Lord lack no good thing. (Psalm 34:10)

I seek the Lord, so I will not lack any good thing. Success is no doubt a good thing. Philippians 4:13 says I can do all things through Christ Who strengthens me, so I will not fail. Failure is not our lot.

The Response to Poverty

Is poverty welcome in your home? It isn't in mine. Some people love poverty. 2 Corinthians 8:9 states that Jesus became poor so that I could become rich. I am not going to let Jesus suffer in vain.

> And my God will meet all your needs according to his glorious riches in Christ Jesus. (Philippians 4:19)

The Scripture also implies poverty has no place with God's children:

Arresting
the Arrester

The Spirit himself testifies with our spirit that we are God's children. Now if we are children, then we are heirs – heirs of God and co-heirs with Christ, if indeed we share in his sufferings in order that we may also share in his glory. (Romans 8:16, 17)

As heir, whatever your father has belongs to you. And God says in Haggai 2:8, *"The silver is mine, and the gold is mine,' declares the Lord Almighty."*

However, as long as you are willing to tolerate poverty and do nothing to get out of it, you will remain poor.

The story in 2 Kings 4:1-7 of the widow of a prophet is a good example. She had two sons and a huge debt. One day the creditors came calling. When this happened, she resolved to reject poverty. She ran to the man of God and cried for help. Before that day ended, she got enough money to pay her debt and enough money for the rest of her life.

The Response to Despair

Should despair or hopelessness come knocking at your door, what will you say? You must tell despair that it, too, has backed up the wrong road.

To them God has chosen to make known among the Gentiles the glorious riches of this mystery, which is Christ in you, the hope of glory. (Colossians 1:27)

Here's another verse that confirms that despair doesn't belong to you:

Tell the righteous it will be well with them, for they will enjoy the fruit of their deeds. (Isaiah 3:10)

No matter how terrible the situation may be today, do not open the door to despair. If you do, you will die. On the other hand, if you refuse to accept despair, the Almighty God will bring you out of it. It doesn't matter how you feel . Tomorrow is going to be better. Our King says you should be of good cheer because He has overcome the world. Weeping may endure for a night, but joy comes in the morning. Just as you are about to lose hope completely, the Hope of the hopeless will come.

The Response to Fear

If fear comes knocking at your door, tell fear that it has gone off tracks:

> The Lord is my light and my salvation—whom shall I fear? The Lord is the stronghold of my life—of whom shall I be afraid. (Psalm 27.1)

Don't let fear destroy you. There's no need to be afraid. If you have given your life to Jesus Christ, and you stay away from everything that can foul up your life, and you maintain a relationship with the Lord, no evil will come near you. The Almighty God has promised that He will help us (Isaiah 41:10-13). God is in control. God has a plan for you, and the plan is beautiful. It doesn't include fear.

One of the greatest problems many people have is doubt. When doubt comes to you, tell it that as far as you are concerned, it has missed its way. The Word of the Lord is settled forever.

If trouble comes knocking, tell it that it has backed up the wrong road. Jesus Christ is the Prince of Peace, and where He

Arresting
the Arrester

lives, there is no room for trouble.

Lay Your Cares on Him

Now you know how to lead problems in the other direction. But it is not enough to tell problems that they have missed their way when they come to us. In addition, you must tell them where to go. I used to say sickness should go back to the devil, but the Lord said this was wrong. He said I should send sickness to Him.

So send all your problems to Jesus. Before your sickness gets to Jesus Christ, He will deal with it with His stripes. If poverty comes, send it to Jesus, and the One who owns the earth and the fullness thereof will swallow it up (Psalm 24:1). If death comes, send it to Jesus, and it will discover that Jesus has swallowed death in victory. (1 Corinthians 15:54). He is the Resurrection and the Life. If demons come your way, send them to Jesus. In Matthew 8:28, 29, Jesus Christ is referred to as the Tormentor of demons. If failure finds your door, send it to Jesus, and it will soon discover that with God, nothing shall be impossible.

Not only did Elisha say the army had missed its way, but he offered to lead it to the man it wanted. Elisha led the Syrian army to Samaria. They came to arrest him, but he arrested them. They came to take him to their king, but he took them to his King. He turned the table against the enemy. If you take all your problems to Jesus, He will turn the table on your enemy, and He will do it instantly. In Luke 5:1-7, Jesus reversed Peter's failure to catch fish instantly. He succeeded so much that he was amazed. In Luke 7:12-16, God raised the son of the widow of Nain instantly. Sorrow, death, failure and despair all visited her, but Jesus Christ stepped in, and in a jiffy, she was lifted from the bottom of sorrow to the greatest heights of joy.

Under Arrest

To arrest your arrester, you have to do these five things:

(1) Surrender completely to God. Leave your life in His hands. This will give you peace of mind. James 4:7-8 admonishes us to submit ourselves to God and then to resist the devil and he will flee from us. We also are told that if we draw near to God, He will draw near to us. This was true in Elisha's life. The moment God called him, he entrusted his life to God and he surrendered to God. You cannot overcome if you do not totally surrender to God.

(2) Focus on God, not on the enemy. Hebrews 12:2 instructs us to do so: *"Let us fix our eyes on Jesus, the author and perfecter of our faith, who for the joy set before him endured the cross scorning its shame, and sat down at the right hand of the throne of God."*

Psalm 121 2 reveals the benefit of focusing on God:

> *I lift up my eyes to the hills—where does my help come from? My help comes from the Lord, the Maker of heaven and earth.* (Psalm 121:1, 2)

When you focus on the enemy, you lose your peace. You end up distrustful. Everybody near you becomes a suspect. You will have no friends anymore, and you will become isolated. You will have no peace.

God wants you to focus on Him. Elisha's servant focused on the enemy, while Elisha was at peace because he knew he belonged to God. He knew God would not allow any enemy to hurt him. When Peter walked on water, as long as he looked at Jesus, he was afloat. The moment he took his eyes off Jesus,

Arresting the Arrester

the waves drowned his faith, which kept him afloat, and he began to sink.

(3) Be confident. If you have absolutely surrendered to God and your focus is on God and not your problem, it becomes easy for you to be confident. You will know you are not alone, just as Elisha knew. Be confident because the battle is no longer yours. When you have realized this, you will be able to say, as David said to Goliath in 1 Samuel 17:47, that the battle is the Lord's. If the Lord is the One fighting your battles, you already have won.

(4) State specifically, calmly and firmly, step by step, what you want God to do to your enemy. When you have surrendered to Him, you are focusing on Him, and your confidence is in Him, then God says we can command Him to do things (Isaiah 45:11). Elisha did this when he specifically told God to make his enemies blind. As soon as he gave this command, they became blind.

Those who dominate are never domineering. Whenever you see a Christian threatening a demon, you should know that the person doesn't know the basics of deliverance. When you speak with confidence to demons, they will obey.

(5) Praise God in return. God expects songs of praises from us. Songs of praises are our greatest weapons in spiritual warfare. God inhabits the praises of His people. As you praise the Lord, He will arise, and your enemies, which are also His enemies, will scatter. Paul and Silas sang high praises to God in the prison, and their yokes were broken. The one guarding them received salvation and became their servant. They arrested their arrester.

Chapter Eleven

Your Victory is

Permanent

When you have achieved victory over your enemy, the power of God Almighty makes the victory permanent.

The enemies did not come after Elisha again:

> After they entered the city, Elisha said, 'Lord, open the eyes of these men so they can see.' Then the Lord opened their eyes and they looked, and there they were, inside Samaria. When the king of Israel saw them, he asked Elisha, 'Shall I kill them, my father? Shall I kill them?' 'Do not kill them,' he answered. 'Would you kill men you have captured with your own sword or bow? Set food and water before them so that they may eat and drink and then go back to their master.' So he prepared a great feast for them, and after they had finished eat-

Arresting
the Arrester

ing and drinking, he sent them away, and they returned to their master. So the bands from [Syria] stopped raiding Israel's territory. (2 Kings 6:20-23)

As God did when Elisha asked Him to make the army blind, God once again responded positively to Elisha's prayers to open their eyes.

Earlier, Elisha prayed that God would open the eyes of his servant and friend. Here he asked God to open the eyes of his enemies. What is the difference between these two prayers? When he asked God to open the eyes of his servant, it was so the servant would see the superiority of the Lord. David asked the Lord in Psalm 119:18 to open his eyes that he might see the wonders in His laws. When the Lord opens the eyes of friends, it is to see the wonders of God. In the case of his enemies, it was so they would see how vulnerable they were.

The enemies did not know where they were taken until they arrived in Samaria because they had been spiritually blindfolded. But then Elisha wanted them to see so they would know they were in grave danger. In what kind of danger can a believer's enemy be? Your enemy may not know that God had already decreed that no one should touch or harm His anointed:

> He allowed no one to oppress them; for their sake he rebuked kings: 'Do not touch my anointed ones; do my prophets no harm.' (Psalm 105:14, 15)

Evildoers may not be aware of this. Those who are trying to kill you or make you unhappy may not know that God already said that they should not touch you. When God opens their eyes, they suddenly realize they had been trying to hurt the anointed of God.

When God arises in your defense, then the opposition will grasp what the Bible states in Hebrews 10:31, that it is a dread-

ful thing to fall into the hands
of the living God. And anyone
who touches the anointed of
God may fall into the hands of
God. Hebrews 12:29 states that our God is a consuming fire.
In Zechariah 2:5, the Bible states that God surrounds His own
with a wall of fire. If your enemy knows you are surrounded
by fire, he will leave you alone.

Until God opens the eyes of your enemies, they will not realize that now that you are born again, you are the property of
the Lord of hosts. The Lord of hosts will always defend His
own. Some of your enemies may know that you are now the
property of the Lord of hosts and that He will defend you, but
the devil may use them to attack you. Only if God opens their
eyes will they discover that a single angel can destroy 185,000
soldiers in one night.

God opened the eyes of Elisha's enemies, and they realized that
they were in Samaria. They suddenly understood Proverbs
14:12: *"There is a way that seems right to a man, but in the end it
leads to death."*

The Syrian army followed Elisha in what they thought was the
right direction. They didn't know they were heading for
destruction. They also found that the man they had been following was the man they wanted to arrest. Suddenly, it
dawned on them that if God is *for* somebody, nobody can be
against that person. They discovered that if you are pursuing a
man of God, you might find yourself in the midst of the Red
Sea.

They thought they had Elisha, but little did they know the
truth in Isaiah 49:

> Can plunder be taken from warriors, or captives res-
> cued from the fierce? But this is what the Lord says: 'Yes,
> captives will be taken from warriors, and plunder
> retrieved from the fierce; I will contend with those who

91

Arresting
the Arrester

*contend with you, and
your children I will save. I
will make your oppressors
eat their own flesh; they
will be drunk on their own blood, as with wine. Then all
mankind will know that I, the Lord, am your Savior,
your Redeemer, the Mighty One of Jacob.'*

(Isaiah 49:24-26)

No matter how mighty your enemies may be, they are not the
Almighty. The Almighty is mightier than anyone else, and the
Most High is higher than anyone else. This is why His Word
states that at the Name of Jesus, every knee shall bow
(Philippians 2:10).

Different Kinds of Authority

There are many different kinds of authority in the Bible that
can help drive and keep away the enemy.

Political authority is recognized by God.

> *Everyone must submit himself to the governing author-
> ities, for there is no authority except that which God has
> established. The authorities that exist have been estab-
> lished by God. Consequently, he who rebels against the
> authority is rebelling against what God has instituted,
> and those who do so will bring judgment on themselves.
> For rulers hold no terror for those who do right, but for
> those who do wrong. Do you want to be free from fear
> of the one in authority? Then do what is right and he
> will commend you. For he is God's servant to do you
> good. But if you do wrong, be afraid, for he does not
> bear the sword for nothing. He is God's servant, an
> agent of wrath to bring punishment on the wrongdoer.*

(Romans 13:1-4)

Nobody can get to any position of authority without the permission of God. Nothing happens behind His back. Daniel states this clearly:

> *The decision is announced by messengers, the holy ones declare the verdict, so that the living may know that the Most High is sovereign over the kingdoms of men and gives them to anyone he wishes and sets over them the lowliest of men.* (Daniel 4:17)

Psalm 75:7 also affirms that:

> *But it is God who judges: He brings one down, he exalts another.*

There is also financial authority. Ecclesiastes 7:12 states:

> *Wisdom is a shelter as money is a shelter, but the advantage of knowledge is this: that wisdom preserves the life of its possessor.*

Money is a defense. I pity those who say they don't want to hear about prosperity. I pity anybody who talks about nothing but prosperity. I pity anyone who preaches everything but prosperity. I am going to prosper. Poverty is a terrible thing.

> *The wealth of the rich is their fortified city, but poverty is the ruin of the poor.* (Proverbs 10:15)

> *The rich rule over the poor, and the borrower is servant to the lender.* (Proverbs 22:7)

Your prayer should be that poverty should be a stranger to you.

Arresting the Arrester

In addition, there is mental authority. This is also confirmed in Ecclesiastes 7:12, which states that wisdom is a defense and it preserves the lives of those who have it. Wisdom is better than strength (Ecclesiastes 9:16).

How much better to get wisdom than gold, to choose understanding rather than silver! (Proverbs 16:16)

Mental authority is superior to financial authority. With your mental superiority, you can turn a desert into a flourishing land. Wisdom is better than gold. Unfortunately, Ecclesiastes 12:12 also admonishes:

Be warned, my son, of anything in addition to them. Of making many books there is no end, and much study wearies the body.

Wisdom is wonderful; therefore we must study. However, if all you are doing is studying, and you do not learn to walk with God, you will soon discover like Solomon said, that the wisdom of the world has a way of wearing the body out. As you study, make sure you study the Word of God, too. Mental authority becomes effective when you come face to face with Satan, and the only way to defeat him is by referring to the Word of God. If you don't know what is written in God's Word, how will you use it?

Higher than all the other authorities is spiritual authority. The king of Israel recognized this, and that was why he called Elisha his father.

I have given you authority to trample on snakes and scorpions and to overcome all the power of the enemy; nothing will harm you. (Luke 10:19)

Spiritual authority is rooted in the Name of Jesus, which is recognized in heaven and on earth. Through this Name, you can cast out demons, and lay hands on the sick, and they will recover (Mark 16:17, 18). With this Name, you shall decree a thing, and it shall be established (Job 22:28). In John 14:14, Jesus said if you ask anything in His Name, He will do it. The beauty of spiritual authority is in the way you can multiply its effectiveness just by agreeing on any issue with another person with spiritual authority. The moment two people agree on anything, there is nothing on earth that can stand in their way.

> *Again, I tell you that if two of you on earth agree about anything you ask for, it will be done for you by my Father in heaven.* (Matthew 18:19)

Promotion

The Holy Spirit was at work on this issue of the king of Israel calling Elisha "father." Elisha was a former farmer's boy who became the father of a king. This was because the Almighty God promoted him. The Bible reveals that promotion is from the Lord. There are different kinds of promotions. An infertile woman who gives birth to twins has been promoted. The day a bachelor marries, he is promoted. The day a person who had no car buys one, he or she is promoted. The tenant who becomes a landlord has been promoted.

Divine promotion is not always an event. Many times, it is a process. For example, Joseph started out as his father's favorite son, and from there, he became a slave. Then he became a prisoner and later a prime minister. David started as a shepherd boy and soon became a fugitive, running from Saul. Then, he became a king. After being a farmer's boy, Elisha later

Arresting
the Arrester

became a servant to an itinerant prophet. Later he became someone who was called "father" by a king. Peter started as a fisherman and soon became a disciple of Jesus Christ. He then became somebody who could heal by contact. Then he moved up to become somebody whose shadow could heal the sick.

When God begins to promote, there is no limit to how far He will take you. Promotion is of the Lord, but He does it in His own way. If He wants to make you a leader, He will first train you as a servant. If you don't know how to follow, you will not know how to lead.

When we are seeking to keep away the enemies, we must ask God what He wants us to do with them. Proverbs tells why:

> *For waging war you need guidance, and for victory many advisers.* (Proverbs 24:6)

The Response to the Enemy

Elisha listened to God when the king asked Elisha whether he should smite the enemies. The prophet responded by saying no. When God comes face to face with His enemies, He responds one of three ways.

First, He wipes them out, as in Exodus 14:28. Every soldier and chariot of Pharaoh drowned in the Red Sea.

Second, He humiliates them and subdues them, as He did to the enemies (the Gibeonites) who deceived Joshua in Joshua 9:3-21.

Third, He could transform His enemies to friends, as in the story of Saul of Tarsus, better known as Apostle Paul (Acts 9:1-15).

It is one thing to be given good advice; it is another thing to accept it. Elisha said the enemies should be fed, and the king of Israel fed his enemies. The king of Israel accepted Elisha's advice, even though he was more politically qualified to deal with the situation. Feeding the enemies was a magnanimous thing to do. If you will allow God, He will lift you so high above your enemies that you will feed them. It is said that your enemy must be terribly hungry to eat food from your kitchen. It is a sign of your indisputable victory.

When God gives you counsel, accept it. If you destroy all your enemies, you may end up destroying your future friends. Your prayer should be that God would destroy your enemies that are due for destruction, subdue those that need to be subdued, and transform those that are fit to become your friends.

As you listen to the counsel of God, be apprised of Proverbs 12:15, which states:

> *The way of a fool seems right to him; but a wise man listens to advice.*

Where is the counsel of God? It is in the Bible. Many things in the Bible do not make sense to people, particularly those who are highly educated. It was a long time before I could tithe. I knew one hundred dollars was more than ninety dollars, and it was not even enough. It took a long time for me to understand, and God was merciful to me. God persuaded me to tithe, and my life hasn't been the same since. When you accept the counsel of the Lord, you will experience success way beyond your wildest imagination.

This is the promise in Genesis 12:3. God promised Abraham that He would bless those who bless him and curse those who curse him. In other words, whoever sends blessings to you will be blessed. Conversely, if somebody sends a curse to you, the

Arresting
the Arrester

curse will go back to the person. The promise was made to Abraham, but the Bible makes it clear that we are of the seed of Abraham and whatever is true for Abraham is true for us. (Galatians 3:29).

After the enemies were fed and sent back to their king, the Bible recalls that the Syrians never came into the land of Israel again. If you can be patient enough and let God solve your problems in His own way, the solution will be permanent. If you are not in a hurry, the solution of the Almighty God is always a permanent solution. We thank God for doctors, but they don't heal permanently. God heals permanently. He healed me of malaria fever some twenty-three years ago, and it has not returned since then, and it is not going to return. Your miracles also will be permanent in Jesus' Name.

An example is when Elijah decided to burn the soldiers sent to arrest him (2 Kings 1:9-13). He burnt the first set of soldiers, and when another set came, he reduced them to ashes. Yet another set came. If God had not intervened, this could have continued for some time. When God dealt with the whole army that came to arrest Elisha, they never came back. In Exodus 14:28, when the Almighty God drowned Pharaoh's army, they never returned to torment the children of Israel.

According to 2 Kings 5:9-14, the leprosy of Naaman never came back. The Bible recalls that when he dipped himself in the Jordan River seven times, he came out with his skin as soft and smooth as a child's. He never had cause to suffer from leprosy again.

Also, in 2 kings 2:22, the curse pronounced on Jericho's water, which was broken by Elisha, never returned.

In addition, 2 kings 4:1-7 tells the story of the widow who was so poor that creditors wanted to send her sons into slavery. But when God decided to solve the problem, poverty never came back into her life. She never borrowed or begged again.

Conditions for Permanent Victory

There are three prerequisites for permanent victories. First, any victory God has given us will be permanent, as long as we don't fall back into sin. This is illustrated in John 5:1-14, which tells the story of the man who had been sick for thirty-eight years when Jesus healed him. After this, the man went into the temple rejoicing. Jesus met him there and warned him to sin no more so a worse tragedy wouldn't befall him.

Second, keep yourself forever clean from evil forces. Your body that is the temple of the Holy Spirit must be filled with the Holy Spirit and be filled with the Word of God. You must study the Bible and find a fellowship, which can help you grow in the Word. Matthew 12:43-45 explains that if an unclean spirit leaves a man, he scouts around for new spiritual accommodations. On the prowl, he meets other demons looking for accommodations. So together they check out their former "possessions." If they find any that are spiritually vacant, they simply regain residence.

The third prerequisite for permanent victory is found in Psalm 23:

> *Surely goodness and love will follow me all the days of my life, and I will dwell in the house of the Lord forever.*
> (Psalm 23:6)

The only reason why goodness and mercy shall follow you is if you dwell in the house of the Lord forever. Make up your mind and make a covenant with God that you will stay wherever He asks you to stay and do whatever He asks you to do so that together, you can defeat the enemy in your life and your victory will be permanent.

About the Author

Enoch Adejare Adeboye became the General Overseer of The Redeemed Christian Church of God in 1981. The church has experienced unprecedented growth since he became its spiritual and administrative head. Under his leadership, the church hosts a monthly prayer vigil on the first Friday of every month at the headquarters in the Redemption Camp, on the outskirts of Lagos, Nigeria, attracting about 500,000 people per session. Similar meetings are held bi-annually in the United Kingdom and the United States, where the Church has a strong presence.

Also in the eighties, God led Pastor Adeboye to establish "model parishes" that continue to bring young people into the Kingdom in large numbers. The church now has over two million members in about four thousand parishes all over the world.

Pastor Adeboye, a mathematician who holds a Ph.D. in hydrodynamics, lectured at the University of Lagos, Nigeria for many years. He is also a prolific writer of many titles used by God to touch lives. He is married to Pastor Foluke Adeboye and they are blessed with four children.